Did I Say That Out Loud?

ALSO BY KRISTIN VAN OGTROP

Just Let Me Lie Down:
Necessary Terms for the Half-Insane Working Mom

Did I Say That Out Loud?

MIDLIFE INDIGNITIES AND HOW TO SURVIVE THEM

Kristin van Ogtrop

Little, Brown Spark
New York   Boston   London

Little, Brown Spark
Hachette Book Group
1290 Avenue of the Americas, New York, NY 10104
littlebrownspark.com

First Edition: April 2021

Little, Brown Spark is an imprint of Little, Brown and Company, a division of Hachette Book Group, Inc. The Little, Brown Spark name and logo are trademarks of Hachette Book Group, Inc.

The publisher is not responsible for websites (or their content) that are not owned by the publisher.

The Hachette Speakers Bureau provides a wide range of authors for speaking events. To find out more, go to hachettespeakersbureau.com or call (866) 376-6591.

Versions of the following essays were originally published in *Time* magazine: "Don't Make Me Rate You" (May 30, 2016); "How I Learned to Stop Worrying and Love the Roomba" (April 10, 2017); "Facebook? Check. Twitter? Check. Instagram? Check. Snapchat? I Give Up" (March 7, 2016); "My Own Style of She Shed: More Vodka, Less Gingerbread Trim" (originally titled "My Very Own 'She Shed,'" July 6/July 13, 2015); "What This 'Good Enough' Mother Learned from an Extraordinary Babysitter" (August 1, 2016); "Letter of Apology to a Son Graduating from College" (April 24, 2017). "Rebel Love" previously appeared, in a shorter form, in *Adirondack Life* (January/February 2019).

The poem "If You Are Holding This Book" is reprinted with permission from *Dog Songs,* copyright 2013 by Mary Oliver, published by Penguin Press. The poem "Heaven" is reprinted with permission from Patrick Phillips.

A few names and identifying details have been changed to protect the privacy of individuals and enable the author to still have friends.

ISBN 978-0-316-49749-7
LCCN 2020943154

Printing 1, 2021

LSC-C

Printed in the United States of America

For my parents,
who experienced much of this stuff before I did
but never really complained about it

Contents

Contents

Contents

Did I Say That Out Loud?

Just Happy to Be Here!

Something happened in the past few years, something sneaky and silent that I didn't even realize was a problem until it was right upon me, like a bat about to fly into my hair: everyone around me became mindful.

When you were a kid, did you worry about mindfulness? Of course not. You just did your thing, tra-la-la-ing through life, with a relatively mindless approach that usually worked just fine. Now, suddenly, people are paying so much attention! Greeting every situation with open hearts and discerning minds, bidding each other *namaste* everywhere they go. And "learning" how to breathe, which, last time I checked, generally doesn't need to be taught?

As soon as I noticed this awful development I thought, *Ugh. It all sounds so boring and I definitely do not need to change the way I breathe in order to be a better person or find out whether my life has meaning.*

But one of the hallmarks of middle age is the mistaken belief that if you constantly endeavor to keep up with trends, you will never be left behind by your children, the culture, or that one woman in your book group who has always been cooler than you. I am nothing if not middle-aged, meaning it's a long, pitiful slog from now until the end of my days to try to keep a grip on our world as it inexorably advances beyond my reach.

Which is why I found myself, not long ago, in a mindfulness meditation class on an otherwise ordinary Sunday afternoon. I was sitting cross-legged on an orange bolster on the floor of the local yoga studio, trying to accept with an open heart and discerning mind the fact that both of my feet were beginning to fall asleep and wondering whether mindfulness was a bunch of hooey, just as I suspected, when I heard the instructor say, "There is a big difference between *thinking* and *thoughts.*" Immediately I knew that the twenty-five dollars I had plunked in the basket outside the studio was completely worth it because, even if I never achieve mindfulness, that one simple phrase uncovered an essential truth that has eluded me for some time: I used to think, and now I have thoughts.

Oh, there is a difference. Thinking is linear, with one idea leading to another like identical cars of a long train, sleek and shiny, all linked and moving forward with precision to a preset destination. Maybe you are thinking about what you need from the grocery store or whether your dog has to go to the vet or how to reorganize your closet so each item inside doesn't look like something you never want to wear again. Whatever the case, you are progressing in an orderly fashion with the hope—in fact, the reasonable expectation— that when you reach your destination, it will be pleasing and well worth the trip.

Once you pass the age of forty-five, however, the mysterious process happening inside your head is no longer linear. Now you are on a different train, a rickety circus train that looks like it's held together with paper clips. There's an elephant in one car and a lion in the next and then one with a giraffe whose head sticks out of the top and after that a car with a bunch of drunk clowns. You don't know where you're going and, really, does it matter? Because your circus train is probably about to crash.

That is the difference between thinking and thoughts.

Being a person with thoughts isn't all bad. If you lose yourself in the colorful scatter that is your mind, you can find hours of entertainment. But if you fight it—try to get the giraffe to keep his head inside the train or command the clowns to sober up—you are just going to be angry and sad for the rest of your life, however long that might be.

My mindfulness meditation class ended at 5:15 and dinner guests were due to arrive at 6:30. I had worked throughout the afternoon to prepare for the party, making quinoa salad and cutting the asparagus and chilling the wine and setting the table so all I had to do was roast the salmon and asparagus. We were hosting two couples—my friend David and his girlfriend, plus newlyweds who had just moved to town—so with me, my husband, and two of our kids, that made eight people for dinner.

Everything went according to plan and I was feeling mildly triumphant when we all sat down at the table, me on one end and my husband on the other. There was a weird emptiness that I couldn't quite put my finger on, plus a moment of confused silence. Then David said, "Are we expecting more people?" And all at once I understood the reason everyone felt so far away: I had set the table for ten instead of eight.

Ten place mats, ten plates, ten pressed white napkins, ten forks, ten knives, ten water glasses. Ten dessert plates waiting expectantly on the counter in the kitchen. All extremely organized. But not.

We had planned this little dinner party weeks earlier, and the number of people had never changed. Do I remember counting the guests in my head as I dusted the dining-room table and put down the place mats? No. Suddenly my mind was just at ten, because that's where my train of ragtag thoughts had come to rest after it careered over the edge of the cliff.

"Do you want to join us?" David said, and I moved my seat to be closer, and we all laughed and made jokes about the imaginary guests who hadn't shown up. We left the two extra place settings on the table. Everyone stayed a bit too late, which is always a good sign, and I imagine that as David and his girlfriend got ready for bed that night, one said to the other, "Well, that was fun, but it's too bad about Kristin."

When the father of my friend Rob was on his death-bed, he asked Rob, "What's more important, thoughts or feelings?" Rob's dad was eighty-eight when he died, and the closer I get to that number, the more I begin to think that the question he posed was the most interesting question of life. Thoughts are important but they're unreliable, unpredictable, and often un-productive no matter how mindful you are. Feelings, though—feelings are what endure.

This book is for anyone who has lost things over the years—and perhaps you've lost more in this past year, during the coronavirus pandemic, than in all the years leading up to it. If that is the case, I am so sorry.

Hopefully your sense of humor is still intact. Hopefully you know that it doesn't matter if your thought train is headed over a cliff, because it's the feelings that linger when the train is upside down with its wheels spinning in the air. This book is for you if you're someone who knows that setting the table for two imaginary people may be a sign of cognitive decline—or proof that you're a generous person with a welcoming attitude toward her fellow man. Who looks at the indignities of midlife (sleepless nights, elderly parents, a house full of crap you no longer need, not knowing how to dress, adultish children who persist in finding new ways to worry you—should I go on?) and thinks, *Consider the alternative*. Who possesses grace and patience and wit when faced with these indignities, because you have gained perspective by watching terrible things happen to people you love and your catalog of sadness has grown quite thick. You are old enough to have heard stories of unfathomable grief, and you never forget any of them, even as more accumulate over the years: a terminal diagnosis, a child with mental illness, the failure of a love that was supposed to last a lifetime, a global pandemic. You carry these stories with you, thinking, *Consider the alternative*.

You no longer believe you are special, which is a relief. When you're young, it's the job of your parents—

if your parents are good ones—to convince you that there's no one quite like you in all the world and that you are capable of anything your spectacular brain can dream up. Making you believe such a thing might be love, or it might be pressure disguised as love. As you get older, though, you realize that the world is full of people exactly like you. Maybe your hair is thinner or your hips are wider or you have more money or a laugh that lights up the room whenever anyone hears it. Still, you are pretty much like everyone else, which makes you more forgiving. More understanding. It allows you to see that everyone around you is beset with frailties and blessed with strengths, just as you are. Even if—like me—you don't really know how to be mindful, the understanding and forgiveness you now possess make you a kinder person.

And the insignificant worries in your rearview mirror—you are thrilled to watch them diminish. If your children have reached their twenties, you no longer care about where anyone goes to college. Oh my God, the brain cells I burned obsessing over where everybody was going to college! I want all of those brain cells back. This book is for women who have watched enough kids get into and then go all the way through college to know that where you go to college doesn't matter very much. Skinny thighs—

those no longer matter. Also not important: watching that Netflix show everyone is talking about; whether or not your high-school boyfriend would still find you attractive; if your neighbor didn't wave hello because she didn't see you or because she secretly detests you. You are now self-actualized, meaning you don't give a rat's ass. Finally!

When I was in my late thirties I bought a house from a kooky seventy-year-old woman who wore ribbed white tank tops without a bra and left a big messy pile of old family photos on the floor of the garage when she moved out. I gathered them in a neat stack, put them in an envelope, and sent them to her, because it was incomprehensible to me that she had left them intentionally. Old family photos have meaning! But that kooky lady knew then what I know now, which is that they don't. Old family photos are just things, and if you're smart, you know to value memories over things, because although both fade, one can live on in your head while the other just ends up at Goodwill or in some grown kid's first apartment covered in water rings because what's a coaster? And so this book is for the woman who has perhaps stopped caring about things. Maybe even about decorating in general. She looks at her dining-room door frame and sighs, not because the paint is chipped but because she remembers the winter her six-year-old ran into it while riding his Big Wheel inside the house every day. Why should she paint over it? Maybe the chipped paint sometimes makes her feel like her life is completely out of control, but more often it makes her smile, because that six-year-old is now eighteen and most of what she knows about his life comes from Venmo. What she wouldn't give to have that boy banging into the door frame again, shouting to her with glee, just for an afternoon.

Yeats knew that things fall apart and the center cannot hold. My center can't hold either, which is why I've got back fat and a muffin top above the waistband of my pants. But I try to laugh, because back fat and a muffin top and chipped paint and imaginary dinner guests are insignificant frustrations. Minor indignities, in the grand scheme. Middle age is full of them. And there are so many things that are much, much worse. None of us knows how life will turn out, and even if we forget everything else (who is Yeats again?), we must not forget that. So let's just feel happy to be here. To cry sometimes, when the occasion calls for it, but to laugh as often as we can—that is enough. Because consider the alternative.

Chapter 1
Fork Lady

It wasn't until the anesthesiologist on call appeared at my bedside that I began to suspect something might be dangerously wrong with me. She was still in her bulky down coat, little flyaways of wispy hair escaping her ponytail, glasses beginning to fog after rushing inside from the cold. Maybe it was the fact that she was out of breath or the fact that she hadn't taken off her coat, or maybe it was because she was the first person since I had arrived at the hospital three hours earlier to use the words *emergency surgery*. She said it in a quiet, reassuring voice, but you can't change the meaning of a phrase like *emergency surgery* just by changing your tone.

After it was all over, a number of people said to me, "You must have been so scared!" I wasn't then, although now when I look down at the giant purple scar, I do feel the remnants of fear. But I feel something else too. By the time we all reach middle age, our bodies are dotted with scars. Most of mine have come from cartoonish mishaps: when I tripped in the kitchen and fell into the stove; when I collided with a branch on the running trail. Dumb but harmless things I did to myself as I pinballed through life. These scars make me feel idiotic, because they send the message *You are a clumsy oaf.* This big, new scar, though, sends a different message: *Guess what, girl—you are mortal!* And so this scar actually makes me feel...lucky.

The pain started on Thursday morning as a funny little humming in my back. It felt like I had tweaked some tiny, insignificant muscle between my shoulder blades that I'd never bothered to learn the name of, and so now it was going to make itself known. I had a breakfast meeting with a man I found vaguely annoying, so by the time I got to my office I had chalked the pain up to carrying a heavy backpack and having to listen to an irritating person in a crowded restaurant with mediocre food and service that was incomprehensibly slow for midtown Manhattan at nine a.m.

At lunch the back pain was still there. I walked over to the Whole Foods on the edge of Bryant Park, which has an enormous salad bar from which I always pick the wrong things. That day I got cold tortellini salad (like chewing on a sponge) and found a stool at the long counter. Next to me was a young pair, clearly coworkers. The man sat mostly silent as the woman complained about her job and the fact that a third (absent) coworker was leaving their company for something better. "I want a new job too!" she said, and I stole a glance at her, hoping she was at least interesting to look at to make up for the fact that everything coming out of her mouth was a twenty-something cliché. Alas, no. As the conversation became more predictable I tried to amuse myself by turning what she was saying into a little millennial haiku:

Mom says I'm the best
So much talent just wasted
I could run this place

In all fairness, my irritation with the girl was probably caused by the back pain, which had begun to spread. Exactly seven seconds after I swallowed each bite of tortellini, I would get a stabbing pain in what I assumed, from its location, was my stomach. I tried pressing my fist beneath my rib cage after I swallowed, which had always worked on pregnancy-related heartburn. This did not help. I was reading on a Kindle as I ate, bent over with one hand in a fist at my stomach and the other holding the Kindle. Not only was this ineffective but it made me look deranged or like I was in the beginning stages of a stroke. Even with a mysterious little pain in my back and a mysterious big pain in my stomach, I still had enough pride that I didn't want to look like I was having a stroke in front of the whining millennial next to me.

As I walked the three blocks back to the office, I argued with myself about whether or not I should go home. But it was a mild early November day and standing up seemed to alleviate the pain. So I went back to work and harangued the office manager about ordering a standing desk for me since everyone knew that sitting was the new smoking and my back pain was all the data we needed to prove it.

When I got home that night, though, I began to suspect this was not a problem a standing desk could fix. The back pain was still there and the stomach pain was worse. Plus, I had chills. I lay on the sofa wrapped in blankets, my sidekick, our black Lab Jill, snoring on my calves, and decided to take the night off from parenting. Perfect Renata, our sons' longtime babysitter, stood in the doorway and stared at me with alarm. "This is not like you," she finally said.

The next morning was no better.

"You should call your doctor," said my son Owen as he headed out the door.

"I might," I lied. Calling the doctor on your first full day of being sick would violate the Just Wait and It Will Go Away approach to health problems that had gotten me to my sixth decade relatively intact. But I knew Owen would worry all day if I told him the truth.

Honestly, I had no idea what was wrong with me. I canceled my morning coffee date and my afternoon lunch date and told the office manager that I was staying home. I watched from the sofa as the dogs chased each other around the dining-room table, and Renata and my youngest son, Axel, and Axel's friend Manu came and went. It hurt to walk and it hurt to eat, so I lay there all day with my Kindle, reading and dozing, petting the dogs from time to time, feeling dependent and ridiculous and slightly sorry for myself as I waited for whatever this was to pass. At five p.m. my friend Nandini showed up at the door. Nandini is Manu's mom and—most relevant to this story—a doctor.

"Hey," I called from my fainting couch. "Can I ask you something?"

17

Nandini leaned in and peered at me with concern. "You don't look good," she said. "I think it might be your gallbladder." Aha! I wasn't fat, but I was fair and female and fertile (I mean, *ish*) and over forty, four of the five risk factors for gallstones, which for some reason I had memorized instead of memorizing the difference between jealousy and envy or who was president of the United States in 1905. Talking to Nandini emboldened me to call my own internist, who told me that if I didn't feel better in the morning, I should head to the emergency room. But which one? Because I live in suburban New York, there are about fifteen hospitals within twenty miles of my house, and if you believe the comments on the local moms' Facebook group, they're all great and they're all horrible. My doctor seemed unsure of which emergency room I should go to, which was definitely unsettling but, I suppose, a discussion for another time.

• • •

Just before my hospital adventure, my husband and I had begun watching the Showtime miniseries *Escape at Dannemora*. Starring Patricia Arquette, Paul Dano, and Benicio del Toro, it tells the real-life story of two inmates who, in 2015, broke out of the Clinton Correctional

Facility in northern New York with the help of one of the prison employees. Arquette plays the accomplice, Tilly; she runs the prison sewing room when she's not giving del Toro's character blow jobs or presenting him with hacksaws hidden in ground beef so he can escape and take her to Mexico for the exciting life she has always deserved. "She is so self-destructive!" I would cry every time Tilly made a bad decision, which was about seven times per episode. There is something fascinating to me about self-destructive people, perhaps because I pride myself on being moderate and sensible. Regular life is complicated enough without hacksaws in the ground beef.

But people who work in an emergency department see self-destructive behavior everywhere they turn. Which might explain why, after he reviewed my CT scan, the ER doctor gave me a long look, scratched his chin, and asked, "Do you chew on chicken bones?" As I was soon to learn, there are people all over the world who intentionally swallow needles and glass and paper clips and other sharp or dangerous objects. So I suppose it made sense for him to wonder whether the problem in my stomach was self-inflicted; just because someone looks like a moderate and sensible woman doesn't mean she doesn't chew on chicken bones just to see what might happen.

"No," I said.

"Your scan shows a foreign body," he said. "It has perforated your stomach. Do you remember swallowing a fish bone?" This was a tricky question. I can usually recall nearly every single thing I've eaten for the past three days. But remembering everything I've swallowed, even by accident—a dog hair? a piece of tissue? a bit of wax along the edge of a sliver of Manchego?—is something else altogether.

"No," I said.

The ER doctor sighed, his shoulders drooping. "I am sending in the surgeon."

On the other side of the privacy curtain to my left was a man who seemed to be on eighty-seven medications; he was surrounded by family members who obsessively deliberated over which toppings to include on the pizza they were going to order later. I'm no doctor, but it didn't sound like there was much wrong with this guy, as he had strong, lucid opinions about pizza and kept telling everyone, in a loud voice, that he was about to get up and walk out to his car. Behind the curtain on my right was an elderly woman accompanied by her adult son, whose sneakered feet I could see if I leaned forward and peeked around. Two EMTs had wheeled the woman in, and the son announced with exasperation that this marked their fourth visit to the ER in a week. He desperately wanted his mother to be admitted to the hospital, which he repeated patiently to each new medical professional who approached. As he described her health history and medications, his mother mumbled in a low voice, the sound unvarying and unbroken, like a delivery truck idling at the curb. "She's talking to someone who isn't there," the son said to the nurse. "She's talking in her native tongue." All I could think was *I hope to God one of my three sons is this good to me in a few decades when I start mumbling in my native tongue.*

In a flurry, the surgeon appeared with an assistant by his side. Dr. Miguel Silva was an extremely kind, trim man with a clipped way of speaking and frank eyes that never looked away when you were talking. "How often do you eat fish?" he asked, pushing down on my abdomen.

"I don't know," I answered, flinching. "A couple of times a week?"

"When was the last time?"

"I had smoked salmon on Thursday," I said, remembering my breakfast with the annoying man and secretly hoping I could blame him for this entire hospital visit.

Dr. Silva shook his head. "That's not it." He repeated what the ER doctor had said, that a foreign body had perforated my stomach, in the back, hence the pain between my shoulder blades. "If you just had a hole in your stomach, we could give you antibiotics and it might heal itself. But"—he poked the index finger of one hand through two fingers of the other—"because you have a foreign body there, your stomach won't heal unless we remove it. I think I should do surgery on you this afternoon to remove whatever it is and put on a patch. We may have to take out a tiny piece of your stomach, but we'll try not to do that." He waited, staring down at me. "What would you like to do?"

My husband, who'd been with me this whole time, was sitting to my left, just behind the head of my bed. I twisted around and looked at him. He is not a medical professional and, as far as I know, has limited experience with foreign bodies. Still, I felt like I needed a second opinion from someone. "What do you think?" I asked.

His response was sensible, if lacking that supportive touch. "Don't look at me," he said.

I turned back to the surgeon. "What would happen if I waited?"

"Well," Dr. Silva said slowly, "you could get—"

Let's pause for a moment for a list of a few words you hope never to hear come out of a doctor's mouth:

- malignant
- obstruction
- tumor
- terminal
- mass
- quarantine
- intensive care
- MRSA
- staph
- complications

. . . and *sepsis,* which was the word Dr. Silva used next.
"I guess we should do the surgery," I said.

Weeks later, my husband told me that he admired
how I'd handled myself in that emergency room. No
crying. No wavering. All forward motion. In his eyes,
I demonstrated immediate acceptance and resolve: *This
thing happened to me, there is a known fix, so let's get
on with it.* He wrongly attributed my quick decision-
making to strength of character in the face of adversity.
What he doesn't know about me, even after twenty-
seven years of marriage, is that I rarely open the little
door in my brain that allows the mismatched thought
marbles rattling around in there to hurtle down the
chute that leads to the section labeled CONSEQUENCES.
If I did, maybe I would not have attempted to lighten

the mood by saying to Dr. Silva, "Why do you look so unhappy?"

And maybe I would have understood exactly what he meant when he responded, "I wish I didn't have to do surgery on you."

After the visit with the wispy-haired anesthesiologist, I was wheeled out of the ER toward the operating room and finally got a look at the devoted son of the woman mumbling in the bed next door. I had so many questions for him! What language was his mother speaking? Did he write her medical history down and keep it in a card in his wallet or did he just know it all by heart? And how could he possibly take his mother to the emergency room four times in a week and still hold down a job? The son appeared to be in his thirties; he had a scarf around his neck and a backpack on the arm of his chair and very nice eyes that regarded me with a mixture of kindness and sympathy. I didn't think I could ask the nurses to let me stay for a chat, so as I rolled by I simply said, "Good luck."

"You too," he replied with a wan smile.

People who weigh consequences might have been expecting several of the things that happened next, but they took me by surprise. The first was that my husband couldn't go with me through the giant swinging doors that led to the operating rooms. As soon as we got off the elevator on the surgical floor, the cranky nurse accompanying us gave him a look that said *Scram, buster*. When she saw the panic in my eyes, Cranky said, "I mean, I guess he could come in, but he'd have to put on one of these," indicating the flimsy, white, head-to-toe, supposedly germ-blocking bonneted jumpsuit thing she was wearing and that she clearly had no desire to provide. I shrugged, so my husband gave me a kiss and told me he'd be waiting outside. Alone on my bed/gurney/humiliation chariot right beside the nurses' station, I listened to Cranky fume about the fact that the ER hadn't sent up the proper forms. Thus, surprise number two: Even though you are in the midst of a life-changing experience, for everyone around you, it's just another normal shitty day. Because it was a Saturday, the surgical suites were empty. The wispy-haired anesthesiologist reappeared and was listening to another anesthesiologist while he yakked animatedly about somebody's wedding. Cranky's voice carried as she continued to complain about the incorrect ER paperwork, which she waved around in the air like a rebel flag. I wanted to say, *Listen, lady, does this really matter? Let's focus on getting me out of here alive.*

Dr. Silva sat at the nurses' station, ignoring the wedding talk and outraged Cranky, and punched something into a computer. He turned the monitor around to face me so I could see my CT scan. In the middle of a sea of black, there was a glowing white object, small but extremely significant, like the little bomb that's going to blow up the entire civilization if Tom Cruise doesn't dismantle it before the timer counts down to zero. I began to cry, just a little, and silently. I was cold and I was tired, but mostly I felt very much alone and unprepared for whatever was going to happen next. I mean, a person gets more step-by-step preparation when she buys an Ikea bookcase than I did before they used God knows how many sharp objects to remove the sharp object that had somehow rocketed through my stomach. "I'm a little scared," I admitted.

Dr. Silva came over to me, smiled, and put a reassuring hand on my arm. "If you weren't, there would be something wrong with you." *Well, there is,* I thought grimly. *There's a bone in my stomach.*

Remember that scene in *The English Patient* when Ralph Fiennes tells Kristin Scott Thomas that the part of her body he most wants to claim is the little concave nook at the base of her neck? He even gives it a name: the Almásy Bosphorus. If you are Kristin Scott Thomas, that body part is alluring and sexy. If you are Kristin van Ogtrop, however, it's precisely where the yakkity-yak anesthesiologist must press—and press really hard, by the way—if you've drunk a gallon of contrast that you might otherwise aspirate when they're putting you under.

So that's my last memory before the anesthesia did its job: Dr. Yakkity-Yak was pressing much too hard, and I was about to die of suffocation.

A few interesting things happened during the next two hours, and although I was present, I missed them. One was that Dr. Silva made a patch for the hole in my stomach with a piece of my omentum. Never heard of the omentum? Everybody has one! It's an apronish thing that wraps around a bunch of your organs, and, amazingly, you can cut out a little piece of it and sew it onto something else. Clearly the human body is just packed with important parts most of us have never heard of. Are there dozens? Hundreds? Does anyone even know? Or is it like the deepest part of the ocean, where there are species no one has discovered yet? Anyway, now that I know about the omentum, I really wish I could see the patch that it provided, because in my imagination it's a rubber doggy door with a sophisticated little lock on the bottom.

Of course, the most interesting thing of all was that, after two hours of effort and three incisions into my abdomen—two small and one, well, *impressive*— Dr. Silva pulled the foreign body out of my stomach. Before I woke up, he strode down the hall, tweezers in hand, to show it to my husband. It was, astonishingly, unambiguously, the sharp end of a tine of a clear plastic fork.

• • •

At the age of fifty-four, I couldn't remember the last time anyone who was not one of my parents described me as "young." But in the hospital I heard it all the time:

"You are young and active, so . . ."

"You are young and fit, so . . ."

"You are young and healthy, so . . ."

I had my last baby a month before my forty-third birthday. The act of nursing my three children has become a soft, comfortable blur of memory to me, part physical sensation and part overwhelming love, each infant boy now indistinguishable from the others. Except for this one detail: By the time I had my third child, I needed reading glasses. And so when I nursed little Axel, I would peer down into his sweet face and tell him, "I adore you so much, but I can't quite make out your features."

Thirteen years later, I wear my reading glasses for much of the day—while reading the newspaper in the morning, reading e-mails during work, reading a novel in bed before I turn out the light. Who wears her reading glasses when she eats? Not me. But if I had—oh, maybe I could have distinguished the sharp, translucent piece of plastic fork from everything else that rode from my plate to my mouth during the meal that put me in the hospital.

So there's the irony: if my eyes were younger, I might not have given so many nurses and doctors the opportunity to tell me how young I was.

To be clear, the piece of plastic in question was not from my fork. I would have noticed and remembered a broken plastic fork and would have spent some time wondering where the rest of that one tine went. A fork with a broken tine would warrant a conversation with my husband and possibly an emoji-filled group text with my two sisters. No, I'm convinced the plastic was mixed in my food somewhere, either at a restaurant (possible) or a takeout place (more likely). People have asked me how one swallows a piece of plastic. Isn't it too crunchy? Well, if you are a woman who eats lots of vegetables and nuts because that's what your mother and your doctor and the media and all your friends tell you to do, you eat many, many crunchy things. I dare you to close your eyes and bite down on a tough piece of kale stem and tell me it couldn't just as easily be plastic.

Besides, people unintentionally swallow foreign bodies all the time. A few weeks after my surgery there was an article in the *New York Times* about an eighteen-year-old professional athlete who unknowingly swallowed the three-inch toothpick that was holding his sandwich together. He had fevers and vomiting and was hospitalized a couple of times, but no one could figure out what was wrong with him. Finally, the doctors did a colonoscopy and saw the toothpick; they removed it, but it had pierced an artery, which had to be repaired. A few days and a couple of surgeries later, the kid woke up in the ICU, then went on to make a full recovery and return to his sport.

Then there was the sit-up lady. A radiologist I know told me about a woman who had intermittent but excruciating abdominal pain whenever she did crunches. When the radiologist and her technician performed an abdominal sonogram, they were baffled by what they saw. "You have a man-made object in your abdomen!" they said. Turned out the woman had swallowed part of the skewer from a dish of chicken satay.

I have now heard stories of people swallowing toothpicks, skewers, bay leaves, and the bristles of a wire grill brush (which happens a lot more often than you might think; if you learn anything from my experience, it's that you must immediately throw out your grill brush). But I haven't heard about anyone else swallowing part of a plastic fork.

•••

On my third day in the hospital, my parents drove from their house in rural Pennsylvania to see me. On the fourth day, Dad said, "I found a plastic fork in my glove compartment and I was going to leave it on your pillow. Would you have thought that was funny?"

"No," I said. "That would not be funny." His face fell, but I don't see how he could have been surprised, given the circumstances. Although I was on the side of the room by the sunny window, I was in a suburban hospital with a nasogastric tube down my throat and a single shower at the end of the hall that looked like it belonged in a youth hostel in Ukraine.

Weeks later Dr. Silva explained that it takes the body a long time to recover from as much anesthesia as I was given. Apparently major surgery really does a number on you, and that's before anyone even picks up a scalpel. I was not myself—not the Kristin who, through years of trial and error, I had come to know— for quite a while. Of course, the first few days were the trippiest. Axel visited me exactly once during my hospital stay, twenty-four hours after the surgery, and did not like what he saw, which was a nodding-off Mom (thanks, Dilaudid!) with a tube in her nose and a needle in her arm and hair that hadn't been washed in days. "I hate hospitals," he said quietly. "It's where people come to die."

"Or get better," my husband said.

Our son smiled, just a bit. But he was unconvinced.

After I got off the heavy drugs, I became grumpier (the NG—that unique torture device meant to punish people who swallow things they shouldn't—is easier to accept when you are in an opioid fog), but my family chose to ignore my foul mood. My husband was steadfast, visiting every night after work, even during a freak early-season snowstorm that gobsmacked New York drivers and turned the five-mile drive from our house to the hospital into a two-hour test of will. Convincing my parents not to make the drive had worked for only about a day and a half, at which point my mother had texted me *WE ARE COMING IN THE MORNING,* the all-caps indicating that she would brook no argument.

When does a parent stop worrying about a child? Never, apparently. And when does a child stop needing the comfort of a parent's presence? Never, absolutely.

How lucky I was! How lucky to be fifty-four years old with two living parents who wanted to sit for hours at a time in the uncomfortable chairs at the foot of my bed, reading on their iPads and quietly conferring with each other about whether to have the soup or a sandwich in the hospital cafeteria. In this, as in so many things that November, the curse of my experience was wrapped in blessings. Especially in comparison to other patients.

By the time my parents arrived, I was on my second roommate. I've heard many complaints about hospitals but I've never heard anyone point out the lack of a formal introduction system when a roommate is foisted upon you. I think you should get some sort of information card, or maybe there should be a heralding of trumpets. But because there is no system, a new roommate just happens, suddenly, like food poisoning or an Amber Alert.

The first roommate was an Irishwoman who seemed weirdly healthy; she lay on her bed fully clothed, scrolling through her phone with French-manicured fingers. When her husband and three young kids came to pick her up at the end of the day, it was sudden pandemonium on the other side of the room.

Mommy, why are you in the bed?
Mommy, can I get in with you?

Mommy, where are your pajamas?

Mommy, Mommy, Mommymommymommy, you're not listening!

MOMMY!

There was a Buzz Lightyear toy gun going off non-stop and an indecipherable rumble that I assumed was the husband trying to get a word in edgewise. And then I understood. My roommate had come to the hospital to get away from her family.

My next roommate was three months shy of her ninetieth birthday and possessed such stoicism and patience that I was reminded, hourly, of what a gigantic complainer I was. Marcella had suffered a heart attack and could not use her legs. She needed oxygen throughout the day and a nebulizer every four hours, and while she was being transferred from another wing of the hospital to our room on the fifth floor, her wallet had disappeared. Compared to hers, my life was a series of good things, punctuated every now and then by something even better. "You are young," she told me one afternoon. "But I'm old. I am ready to go." Every so often, the chipper physical-therapist duo would breeze into our room to try to help Marcella use her legs. "You're doing great!" they would exclaim. "Just a little bit more!" Marcella was mostly silent during these sessions except for when she told them, matter-of-factly and in a low voice, "I want to die." She said it without emotion, but I believed her. I also believed by then that a hospital stay with no clear end date could make even the most optimistic person feel truly hopeless.

On Saturday, before he'd wheeled me into the operating room, Dr. Silva said I would probably be back at work "by the end of the week." To be fair, this was when he thought it was a fish bone in my stomach that he could remove laparoscopically. Once he'd "opened me up" (awful, medieval phrase) to pull out the fork, Silva and his team said I'd most likely have to stay through Tuesday, which somehow turned into Thursday. "We just want to give you more time to heal," everyone said, an explanation I found maddening in its lack of precision.

"Do you like the new beds?" the nurses kept asking breathlessly. It was a ridiculous, rhetorical question, because really, only the nurses were excited about the new beds. The rest of us had never experienced the old beds and couldn't give a flying fuck anyway. My roommate and I just wanted to get out of there, me to my own house, Marcella to heaven. The only thing interesting about the new beds was the model name printed on the frame, which was the same name as the street where I live. I spent the entire week trying to figure out if that was a sign of good luck or its opposite.

When you are in a hospital for an extended stay, certain dependable aspects of your existence begin to lose their meaning. Nighttime, for instance, becomes an abstract, farcical notion. It's true that at nine p.m. the visiting hours end, and at eleven-ish the lights seem to dim. But then, when it's quieter and darker, the screams of the woman in the room next door just seem louder, and even the noise-canceling headphones your husband has kindly provided don't block out that sound, or the sound of the nurse arriving at two a.m. to check your blood pressure, or the rhythmic whine—and, when the bag is empty, the loud beeping—of the IV machine conveniently positioned twelve inches from your head.

When you don't get much sleep for the better part of a week it's hard to tell if your foul mood is due to (a) self-pity, (b) simple exhaustion, or (c) a leaking or bursting or pooling of fluid someplace in your abdomen where fluid doesn't belong. By Thursday I was pretty sure it was (c).

That afternoon I told the physician's assistant making rounds, "I have a persistent pain here on my right side when I press down." I said it as nonchalantly as I could, but two seconds later I was on a gurney heading for another CT scan. They wheeled me through a big waiting room filled with people. There is something terribly humiliating about being pushed through a crowd of strangers while wearing nothing but under-pants and a thin hospital gown. Particularly when the strangers are anxious or bored and each set of eyes follows you as you go by because you provide a few seconds of break from the worry soundtrack looping through their heads as they await the results of the MRI. There was no one else waiting for a scan, but the technician, who seemed like an appealing person based simply on the number of silver bracelets he was wearing, told me they needed to take someone else before me. He stood at the foot of my bed, looking past me and down the hall.

"They think I might have an abscess," I said, hoping he would answer, *Oh, no, that's extremely rare.*

Instead he said, "Or a leak."

"A leak?"

"That's what the order says," he replied uninterest-edly. "An abscess or a leak."

Just then there was a commotion in the hall and a clus-ter of about seven chattering people appeared, all dressed in athleisure, wheeling a woman who lay silent and twisted and oblivious with her gray hair matted against her scalp. I can't imagine how they got her into the CT scanner, but when they returned her empty gurney to the hall, I could see, beside the crumpled sheets, a spot of moisture that had leaked from some orifice in her body.

And then I started to cry. I was sad for the old lady and scared for myself and just so depressed at the thought that one day I would be a woman on a gurney who left a wet spot after some jokers in Adidas tracksuits threw my body into a CT machine with no one to hold my hand or tell a funny story or reassure me that everything was going to be fine.

The technician with the bracelets came out into the hall and pretended not to notice that I was crying. "Are you cold?" he asked.

"Yes," I said.

He brought me a warmed sheet, which was nice. But I still hated him. I continued crying as he did the scan and was sniffling as he wheeled me back out into the hall. Instead of telling me goodbye or good luck or handing me a tissue, he said, "I hope everything turns out okay for you." Which sounded ominous to me. Like he knew the horror movie wasn't over yet, because he'd seen something I hadn't behind the closed door of the bedroom closet, and he knew it was a man with a knife.

● ● ●

When our middle son, Hugo, was in eighth grade, he had appendicitis, which was how I learned that the word *perforate* could be applied to something other than a roll of stamps or a checkbook. An emergency appendectomy was followed by three separate hospital stays involving a post-op abscess, a PICC line, and a temporary drain that traveled from Hugo's abdomen into a bag taped to his leg that, luckily, could be concealed by long shorts when he finally went back to school.

The experience of Hugo's perforated appendix and its aftermath was like trying to get to shore while big waves keep hitting you from behind. You are half crawling and half walking and just when you think you're in the clear, a wave knocks you forward and you're underwater again. The lesson was that medical emergencies don't always have a definitive ending. There's often another wave coming up behind you, and it will take longer than you ever imagined to feel solid ground beneath your feet again. Hugo's appendix odyssey did end, finally, after he spent ten days on the pediatric floor of Columbia Presbyterian Hospital. What didn't end was my maternal regret and guilt—regret's ugly cousin—that we hadn't caught the problem sooner, while his appendix was still intact.

There were many moments after my surgery when it seemed that everything I experienced was just karmic payback for the insufficient parenting of Hugo. Which meant I wasn't entirely surprised when Danielle, the pretty PA with the long brown hair, showed up in my room after the CT scan, perched beside me on a chair, and told me in a sympathetic voice that I had an abscess and couldn't go home. "So," she said slowly, "tomorrow is Friday, and then it's the weekend. You should probably expect to be here through Monday."

Because of the time-bending nature of a hospital stay, Monday felt like it was a year and a half away. I was too defeated by this news to call my parents, who had gone to my house for the evening, or to text my husband, who was still at work. It was just me and a growing self-pity that was threatening to blot out every other feeling in my emotional tool kit. In retrospect, it was one of the defining moments of my adult life. I had two choices: start to cry again and never stop or say, *FUCK IT. I am putting on my slippers.*

I went with the slippers. Screw the nurses who insisted I wear the awful brown hospital socks with the treads on the bottom that tracked crap into my bed every time I put my feet under the covers. I got my real slippers out of my bag, took a shower, put the slippers on, returned to my bed, and slid my bare feet between the sheets. In short, I decided to make myself feel better. And, for the time that was required, it actually worked.

Like many awful events in life, my hospital stay did teach me a few things:

(1) When a doctor starts a sentence but doesn't finish it, it's because the end of the sentence could be *and then you might be dead*. An example: After the surgery, Dr. Silva said of my little plastic fork piece, "It was *very* close to your colon." He looked at me meaningfully, as if I were supposed to know exactly what that meant. He continued, "If it had perforated your colon, well . . . " And then his voice trailed off ominously.

(2) When it's time to take out your NG tube, the doctor will say, "Hold your breath," pull a length of plastic from your body that is so long, you're pretty sure it could have gone all the way down to your big toe, and throw it into the trash can right next to where you are sitting. You try not to look at it, but you can't help it—it's captivating and repulsive all at once.

(3) You raise a child to be independent, meaning in part that he should never worry about you, but if you have emergency surgery and he doesn't appear to be worried enough, then you're mad at him.

(4) A hospital kitchen can make a pureed "waffle" by putting a real waffle in a blender and then pouring it into a waffle-shaped mold that produces something that looks like a mini version of the real thing but is actually a cruel joke. Once the "waffle" makes it to the room of someone who is permitted only pureed food, it sits on the plate like a lonely piece of orange plastic left over from some kid's kitchen set. Although the familiar shape is encouraging, it tastes like something you wouldn't willingly put in your mouth even if you hadn't eaten for six days.

(5) Once a doctor puts you on one drug, you will then make your way through six other drugs, because every drug makes another drug necessary.

- Dilaudid makes you nauseated, so you get Zofran.
- Flagyl gives you headaches, so you get Tylenol.
- Flagyl then gives you a rash, so you get taken off that and put on levofloxacin and clindamycin.
- Levofloxacin and clindamycin give you oral thrush, so you get nystatin.
- Nystatin gives you diarrhea, which means you panic at your sister's house on Thanksgiving and have to call Dr. Silva. "I think I have sepsis," you say. "Sepsis!"

he says, befuddled. "Why would you have sepsis?" "I don't know," you say. "Because I have Google?"

(6) When they need to move your IV from one arm to the other and your adorable nurse can't find a vein, she'll call Dr. Whosiwhatsit. He will come from another floor, find the vein, and transfer your IV, but not before leaving an enormous bloodstain on the pillow he propped under your arm, the kind of bloodstain a nurse would never have casually left behind. Are you expected to keep putting your head on that pillow during the hours known as "night"? Later the dear nurse will give you a new pillow and ask, "How was he?" When you say, "Fine," because why get into it, she will whisper, "He used to be very rude but then they talked to him."

(7) When you swallow something bizarre, people will ask whether you remember the children's rhyme "There Was an Old Lady Who Swallowed a Fly." If you're in the right mood it gives you a kind of sadistic pleasure to remind them that the old lady dies in the end, just to see the mortified looks on their faces.

(8) When you swallow something bizarre, the hospital staff comes up with a nickname for you. Mine was Fork Lady.

(9) Most nurses are friendly and kind and heroic, and if you're in a hospital in New York, it seems like they're all from Jamaica.

(10) If you are an athletic-looking Jamaican male nurse, the father of Fork Lady will ask you if you played football. The father knows that football is not really a Jamaican sport, but he is undeterred. When you say no, he will ask whether you follow the career of New York Giants rookie running back Saquon Barkley, former star of Penn State's football team. In fact, if you are any sort of male standing next to Fork Lady's bed for longer than twelve seconds, her father will ask you about Saquon Barkley. And when Fork Lady's father sees an enormously tall, beefy guy wearing hospital scrubs walking ahead of him in the hall, he will point at him and announce, "He played college football." His wife and daughter will cry, in unison, "Don't talk to him!" And he will reply, "I already did."

And finally:

(11) CT scans can be wrong. While a scan might know that a foreign body has perforated your stomach, it may not know the difference between an abscess and a

harmless, perfectly natural little collection of fluid that resulted from your emergency surgery. Which is why, on Friday morning, after I had accepted the fact that I would be staying through the weekend, the surgeon doing rounds appeared at my bedside and said, "You can go home."

It was a two-and-a-half-hour surgery followed by a six-night stay. I had two roommates, seven drugs, eight visitors, two CT scans, three deliveries of orchids, one surprise batch of brownies from a friend who instructed me to hand them out to the nurses. And a thousand reasons to feel lucky.

When I was in eleventh grade at St. Mark's High School, my English teacher was Mrs. Dorn. She was breathless and fragrant and had a cylindrical body like an oil drum. One assignment for her class was a diary entry, which in my case was pages and pages of misery about the fact that I couldn't get Fred Land to love me. As a middle-aged woman, Mrs. Dorn must have been bemused by the drama and depth of my teenage despair. But she was kind, and when she handed back my assignment, her only comment, penned in her perfect, loopy, parochial-schoolteacher handwriting, was *Time heals.*

I have thought of Mrs. Dorn often over the years, because even though she taught me a cliché, it's a cliché that's true. Time does heal. Eventually the drugs work and the body regains strength and, even though you haven't eaten or slept much in a week, you are better. And then you find yourself standing in the lobby of Lawrence Hospital with your slippers in a bag as you listen to your father tell the valet-parking cashier—who apparently has become his best friend over the course of your stay—"That's my daughter. She swallowed a fork."

A few days after my surgery, my friend Nandini told me, "This could have killed you, you know. People go to bed with sepsis and never wake up." Even though I was fifty-four, the idea that I could die at any moment was something I knew but didn't really *know*. Understanding that I came—perhaps—closer to death than I have at any other time in my life makes me wish I had treated my hospital stay a bit differently. There are four words most of us could stand to say a lot more often: *Thank you* and *I'm sorry*. I wish I had invited about a hundred people to visit me, and I would have said some combination of those words to every single one. I would have thanked my friends for keeping the lights on in my life, my bosses for helping me find my way, my family for everything. I would have issued some heartfelt apologies: to my children for the times I lost my temper instead of taking a deep breath, to my husband for nagging when I should have kept my mouth shut, to my parents for all the years I had taken them for granted, as if they were going to live forever. I would have thanked Marcella, who, in her octogenarian wisdom, reminded me that I had many wonderful days ahead of me. I would have said I was sorry to my annoying, pre-surgery breakfast date—it wasn't your fault after all. And I would have apologized to Mr. DeCario, my seventh-grade Spanish teacher, for that time I saw a picture of his dog and asked if it was his wife. I was just trying to be funny, a lifelong impulse that consistently yields mixed results. *Lo siento,* Señor DeCario.

People describe middle age as a time when you begin to confront your mortality. But sometimes your mortality is there on the curb, waving, and you don't recognize it as you quickly drive by on the way to something else. You see it out the window and it looks vaguely familiar, like a B-list actor or someone you knew a little bit in college, and you are briefly puzzled until your mind turns to other things. Later you may say to yourself, *Oh! I know who that was! Maybe I should have waved back.* Such was my brief career as Fork Lady.

The four-inch scar that runs down my abdomen now is a thing of fascination; it's clear that Dr. Silva had to go around my navel, so the incision line does a little swerve in the middle and looks like half of what I would call a circus if I lived in London or a rotary if I lived in Boston but, since I live in New York, I think of as a traffic circle. Recently I visited my dermatologist, and she begged me to let her give the scar a laser treatment.

"It doesn't bother me," I said.

"Well, it bothers *me*," she said.

What I didn't tell my dermatologist was this: A month after my surgery I went to church, and the penultimate verse of the final hymn contained the refrain *With what rapture, with what rapture, with what rapture gaze we on those glorious scars!* When I look down at my abdomen I do not feel rapture. That would be impossible, with the stretch marks of three pregnancies and a purplish scar cutting through the loose skin like a dull knife through cake icing. But I feel aware. I remember Nandini's words and am thankful that I can see the scar for what it is. Not a flaw. A reminder.

Chapter 2

Don't Make Me Rate You

Last week I had to attend an event that required me to look better than my regular wilted self (I left "effortless beauty" behind somewhere in my twenties), so I did what many self-respecting women would do: I went for a blowout at a nearby Drybar. Drybar is the kind of totally genius, why-didn't-I-think-of-that business that is making someone who is not me very rich. Afterward, my hair looked much better—so much better, in fact, that I was feeling almost effortlessly beautiful until I got back to my desk to find an e-mail from Drybar, asking if I would rate my experience. Which means there's yet another business I have to break up with because it wants more of me than I'm willing to give.

Life is so complicated now, and I'm pretty sure it's Yelp's fault. Before we were all rating and reviewing everything we did, life was straightforward. Now in order to buy, visit, or do anything, you need to follow this six-step process:

1. Decide and plan to do the thing.
2. Do the thing.
3. Take a photo of yourself doing the thing.
4. Post the photo of you doing the thing on social media.
5. Repeatedly check how many likes the post of you doing the thing got.
6. Rate the thing.

Meaning just going to Taco Bell or the dentist becomes a six-step process. And sensible curmudgeons like me would usually like to stop after step 2.

As I see it, there are two problems with our rate-everything way of living. First, the mystery-of-life issue. By my completely unscientific estimation, every time a new social-media platform is introduced, life loses about eighty-five hundred mysteries. Before long we will all know everything about everybody, and most of it will be stuff you didn't want to know in the first place. Ever since Kim Kardashian's naked derriere broke the internet, the idea that we can "leave something to the imagination" has grown more and more remote.

Okay, millennials, I know what you're thinking: consumers expressing themselves through ratings allows businesses to constantly iterate, remain in lean start-up mode, do all those things that sounded super-sexy and new back in, oh, 2009. Well, guess what—I'd venture to say there can be more muscle in keeping your opinions to yourself than in giving a business a lousy review. Have we forgotten that there is great power in holding your cards close to the vest? In cultivating mystery? (J. D. Salinger, help me out here.) Would Mr. Darcy— the most captivating, mysterious man in literature— have rated his Uber driver after being dropped off at Pemberley? "My good opinion once lost is lost forever," he avowed, and I'm not sure anyone wants to know more than that. During my thirties I worked for a woman whose power was all about her inscrutability. Every day involved anxious metaphorical tea-leaf reading on the part of her staff.

"Did she like that thing you showed her?"

"I don't know, she hasn't responded."

"Where did she go all afternoon?"

"I don't know, she didn't tell anybody."

She was stern, capricious, taciturn, and, above all, mysterious, which both explained her allure and enabled her to keep us firmly in her control.

Second problem with rating everything: the time-suck factor. No, Drybar (and Uber and Everlane and Paperless Post), I do not want to be in a committed, dynamic relationship with you. I don't want to fill out a survey, and while I appreciate the peppy e-mail from user-support associate Katie, I resent you for the time I spent reading it. Katie, if I need help, I will reach out. Am I just a grumpy middle-aged lady who left effortless beauty behind in her twenties and now mostly wants to be left alone? Perhaps. And I'm a hypocrite—I often make recipes on the basis of the number of stars they receive and choose movies by Rotten Tomatoes scores.

In summary, and to businesses everywhere: I just want you to provide me with something that I pay for and then I want no contact with you until the next time I need you. Isn't it enough that I gave you my credit-card number? If time is indeed money, then by taking my money and afterward making me rate the experience of you taking my money, you're essentially double-billing me. And I'm pretty sure that's still illegal, at least in most states. All I know is that as soon as I rate the experience of writing this essay, I'm getting on the horn with the FTC.

Chapter 3

I Can Smell My Pillow

I have a close relative who, for reasons I never want to understand, blamed every bad thing that happened to him between 2008 and 2016 on Barack Obama. He took this Obama-blaming to a ridiculous extreme. An example: One summer Saturday we found ourselves on I-93 in New Hampshire; due to construction, there was a traffic jam, so what should have been a thirty-minute drive took us more than two hours. When we finally got out of the car, hot and hungry, my relative said, "It's Obama's fault."

This is how I regard estrogen. Although a woman has fifty hormones in her body, estrogen is the president and right now everything is her fault. Specifically, I feel as if she has abandoned me—which is exactly how I feel about Barack Obama—and I mourn her absence from my life. I can handle a lot of the problems associated with estrogen's departure, and we're not going to get into all of them now. Too sad, too tedious, too gynecological. But the sleep problems are another story.

You wake up somewhere between 1:00 and 5:00 a.m. Let's call it 2:07. Maybe you're having a hot flash or maybe your partner is snoring or maybe there are mice in the walls or maybe God just wants you to be awake for reasons you won't understand until you're dead. You lie there waiting for the arrival of your regular set of worries (looming work deadline, that kid who is a bad influence on your son, whether the pain in your jaw means you need another root canal). These regular worries are consistent and dependable, like old friends, and you know how to handle them. But on this particular 2:07 a.m., you find that your brain is a party that's gotten out of control. Your friends have friends who have friends who have friends who have people they follow on Snapchat, meaning your few reliable worries multiply at a magnificent rate until every worry you've had in the past six months plus every worry you anticipate having in the next six all crowd together in your brain. It's loud and hot and before you know it, someone is throwing up on the living-room rug. Then the police show up.

Today the party started at 3:03, and it went like this:

3:04: There's that load of whites in the washing machine. Must remember to put in dryer before I leave for work.

3:18: Can't forget to click on the e-mail link to have that thing delivered to the house.

3:35: If I spray Bitter Apple on the sheepskin rug that the puppy keeps chewing, maybe I can leave the rug where it is for the day instead of hauling it up to the bedroom and out of her reach.

3:36: Must make Axel brush the dogs tomorrow. Tumbleweeds of hair in the kitchen suggest slip-shod household attitude. Is this what my life has become?

3:41: Ashley hasn't texted me back about baby-sitting next weekend. Is she out of the country? She is awfully well traveled for a seventeen-year-old. Where does the money come from?

3:50: Is it snowing yet? Do I need to wear my

snow boots to work? Where are my snow boots?
Front porch?

4:00: *Oh, screw it.*

I swung my legs over the side of the bed and headed
for the bathroom. My husband raised his head off the
pillow. "You're not getting up now, are you?" he asked.
As if that were a reasonable option for any reasonable
person who wasn't a *Today* show host. When I crawled
back into bed, he put his arm around me. "Try not to
think," he said.

"You used to say 'empty your head.'"

"Yes," he said. "But I no longer believe that's possible."

The alarm was set for 6:05 (my ongoing and often
futile attempt to exercise before work), and I reached
over and reset it to 7:15, although I haven't slept past
7:00 since the last century. Besides, would the seventy
minutes even make a difference? I'd have an easier time
figuring out game theory than solving that one, but it
was worth a shot.

If you are reading this book, you probably aren't
scared that a guerrilla army is going to be camped
out in your front yard in the morning or that your
daughter might be kidnapped by Boko Haram. More
likely than not, you have clean water and a house with

heat. Unless you are a lifelong New Yorker who never learned to drive, you probably have a car you can drive to a grocery store that sells a hundred and fifty kinds of yogurt. Still, your relative good fortune won't keep you from waking up in the night, and it won't make you feel any better in the morning.

Whether it's called *monkey brain* or *insomnia* or something more profane, few of us are spared. You know about good sleep hygiene; you've read all the articles. Maybe you've tried gabapentin or melatonin; you have special reading glasses that filter out the blue light; you keep your bedroom temperature below sixty-five. You have a white-noise machine and earplugs. You never drink more than one glass of wine, even when you go out. And still.

The morning after a terrible night's sleep, you may look the same on the outside, but inside you are a dramatically different person. All the smooth edges are now jagged and there is a Jimi Hendrix guitar solo playing in your head. Coffee doesn't make a dent. Everything around you is either (a) awful, (b) devoid of logic, or (c) much too difficult to attempt. You scowl at your children and snap at your husband and tell the dog you are too grumpy to feed him—the mere fact that he wags his tail as you enter the kitchen annoys you—and nothing-nothing-nothing is appealing, even the idea of going back to bed (as if that were a possibility). So you put extra concealer beneath your eyes and slog through the day.

My Dutch grandmother had an expression: *Ik kan mijn kussen ruiken.* Loosely translated, it means "I can smell my pillow." She would say this at the end of a dinner party as a way to get her guests to leave. After I've had a bad night's sleep, I am chanting *Ik kan mijn kussen ruiken* to myself all day long, and by nine p.m., once I've washed my face and brushed my teeth, I'm so desperate to smell my pillow that I think I might die.

Let's consider why you can't sleep. Is it . . .

- your children
- your pets
- your spouse
- your ex
- your job
- your diet
- your parents
- alcohol
- gluten
- caffeine
- your house
- the news

including your soul—which was once so crisp and defined, slowly turns to sludge. Plus, you get a little fat, and when you stop eating peanut M&M's and take the stairs instead of the elevator, you just get fatter. Last fall I went on a trip with four of my college roommates, women I lived with thirty-five (!) years ago. It was a long, glorious weekend of discovering all the ways in which we have become different and all the ways we are the same. We live in different parts of the country, have very different jobs, and, to a degree, have differing political views. But we all have kids. We're all in long-term marriages. And three of us start each morning with a pretty little synthetic thyroid pill. I was the baby of the group, as I take only 25 micrograms. One of my former roommates takes 150 micrograms, and she is extremely fit, with tons of energy and gorgeous skin. According to my endocrinologist, I will be on this thyroid pill for the rest of my life, which is fine with me. I'm hoping I can work my way up to 150 micrograms and then maybe I will run for president.

I wish I could say that once my thyroid was regulated, everything else fell into place, but it didn't. And, scientifically speaking, Hashimoto's disease does not cause insomnia the way some thyroid disorders do. However, gaining weight and having your soul turn to sludge leads to an existential restlessness that is not conducive to sleep. And so my mind-body connection remains unfathomable, a daily mystery that begins in the wee hours of the morning. Sometimes the exact same wee hour for days at a time. There was a long period when I woke up every morning at 5:35, no matter what time I went to bed. I wish I could hack into the mind-body navigation system that directed me to wake up at 5:35. Why was it always the same time? What did my brain know that the fingers setting the alarm for 6:05 didn't? Did the number 535 have some significance, cosmically or culturally? I couldn't shake the feeling that somewhere, someone was laughing at my expense. Last week at the dinner table my eleven-year-old son asked me if I knew what the number 420 meant. He's in sixth grade! Let's put aside for the moment the concern that my baby is just a blink of an eye away from smoking weed behind the garage while I'm making breakfast. *What does 535 mean?*

There are two benefits to sleepless nights. The first is that being extremely tired makes you feel like you are covered in cotton balls for the entire next day, a soft, springy layer of insulation that makes you not really care all that much about whatever comes your way; the only important thing is that the hours keep moving forward until the moment that you once again smell your pillow. The second is that, after a bad night, you

Chapter 4
Your Children: The Disappointment

The other morning I was standing at the kitchen counter slicing fruit when Owen's friend Carey came over. Carey is practically a member of our family and I am always happy to see him walk in the door. But this time as we made polite small talk it dawned on me, slowly and with horror, that I was still in my pajamas. Carey has witnessed me at my generous best and my harpy worst, every which way (or every *witch* way, as it were), but he had never seen me in my thin cotton pajamas. Meaning dressed in such a way that my breasts, once a perky sign of vitality and life, came to rest somewhere just above my waist, a pair of sad, half-empty water balloons, too deflated to pop if you threw them at anybody. There are a few frightening realities that no twenty-five-year-old friend of the family should be confronted with first thing in the morning, and braless me in cotton pajamas is one of them. I think I burned a hole in Carey's eyeballs.

Although I've been practicing it for more than two decades, parenthood remains full of surprises, some of them even pleasant. When Carey showed up that morning, my mind and breasts were unprepared. Which is exactly what happens when you become a parent. Like so many things in life, parenthood as an *idea*—an idea held only by the childless—is shiny and bright and surprising (in a good way!), full of wonder, a glorious and fundamental part of life's journey. It defines you and sends a signal to the world. Parenthood, the idea, is a new BMW painted a thrilling color of red that beeps when you're about to back into something and features heated seats and a driver's door that automatically unlocks when it detects the presence of a key in your hand. Parenthood, the childless believe, will enhance, fulfill, and complete you.

I am the mother of three sons who are, at this writing, twenty-four, twenty-one, and twelve. My mother has a now-hilarious photo that she likes to reference from time to time, taken when Owen, our eldest, was four days old. It's an image she captured from the kitchen doorway of our Brooklyn apartment looking into the living room, where I am sitting in a wing chair with Owen on a pillow in my lap. I am having trouble breastfeeding, and my husband sits beside me, holding in his hands a copy of *What to Expect When You're Expecting*. I am naked from the waist up and my enormous right breast dominates the photo. Heads together, my husband and I are poring over the book, trying to figure out how to master this simple but mysterious act, while Owen stares at nothing, no doubt wondering whether he could put in a request for less clueless parents. When my mother talks about this moment all these years later, she just laughs and laughs.

Owen and I eventually did figure it out, and while the breastfeeding expertise didn't come from a book, that photo captures something else: the moment we realized that parenthood is not the thrilling red BMW with heated seats. Parenthood is the opposite of luxurious and accommodating. Parenthood is a Tesla sedan with doors so strange, you can't figure out how to open them. Parenthood is a Honda Accord with fabric upholstery that smells like someone else's cigarettes. Parenthood is a Chevy Suburban that's so big, you can never see what's happening in the back. It's a Suzuki with a manual written entirely in Japanese, and you don't understand Japanese. It's a Smart car so tiny, even two passengers feels like too many. It's a noisy school bus with no seat belts. Sometimes it's an ambulance.

There aren't enough words to adequately capture how it feels to become a parent. *Overjoyed* is one. Also *gobsmacked. Inept. Despairing*? And *uncomfortable*, at least in the breast department. Your heart is overwhelmed by a crowd of feelings you never imagined could coexist within a person. And they change by the hour; *highs* and *lows* take on new meaning. You wonder how you ever felt anything at all before now, before you experienced being a parent. Miracles like this do not disappoint—at least, not at first. But slowly, over time, you will learn that the red BMW you thought you were promised by destiny is nowhere in sight. Luckily this realization and the disappointment that accompanies it don't come until later. Which is why so very few people trade their children in.

There are three phases of parenting. By the time parents reach middle age, many of us have passed through the first two phases and have settled, with resignation and relative contentment, into the third.

If there is a fourth phase, I haven't reached it, and probably don't want to know about it.

Parenthood, Phase 1: Your Child Will Be Everything You've Dreamed Of

For those who do it on purpose, having a child is an exercise in narcissism. Making a baby requires you to regard your genetic material highly enough that you're convinced the world needs more of it. Your child, naturally, will be special. If your path to parenthood is straightforward and problem-free, you are grateful. You try not to allow yourself to believe that this happy fate is one you deserve because you are a nice person with a moral compass that usually points in the right direction. Sometimes that ugly little thought creeps in—that if anyone is entitled to a healthy baby, it's you—but you keep it to yourself. You are lucky, and you're not going to push it.

Remember the scene in *Bull Durham* when Kevin Costner says to Susan Sarandon, "How come in former lifetimes everybody's somebody famous? How come nobody ever says they were Joe Schmo?" Susan Sarandon laughs her hearty, half-manic laugh and shakes her adorable curly head of hair and says, "Because it doesn't work that way, you fool!"

Just as you were undoubtedly Joan of Arc or Jane
Austen or Sojourner Truth in a past life, so your
child is destined to be something outstanding in this
one. Everything your new baby does is a miracle,
and even though any infant is, objectively speaking,
pretty boring, you could stare at him all day long.
That's how nature ensured that our species would
survive: by making a homunculus who does nothing all day seem like the most fascinating sight in
the world.

You know with certainty that as your child grows
up, he will remain perfect, and then one day he will
become a famous and successful... well, something or
other. You're fuzzy on the particulars, but he will be
someone spectacular, maybe even like Francis of Assisi,
who is one of the people Susan Sarandon's character—
Annie—thinks she was in a former life. Of course, you
don't really want your child to grow up to be Francis
of Assisi, because that would involve a vow of celibacy
and then who would provide you with grandchildren?
But no matter. Now, if you remember the movie,
Annie is just a weirdo who wears vintage dresses and
devotes most of her unique brainpower and seemingly
unlimited free time to the successes and failures of a
local minor-league baseball team. This is the type of
person who believes not only in remarkable past lives

but also in unlimited human potential, which is why she makes it her mission to seduce baseball players so they can perform better. But you are not Annie. You are the opposite of crazy and irrational. Although you're starting to believe in the unlimited-human-potential thing. Because look how smart your kid is! When he does something amazing, like recognizing a backhoe pay loader along the highway or reciting the last line of the picture book from memory or telling you that red and blue combine to make purple, you think to yourself, *Where did that come from?* And the answer, naturally, is *From me!*

You are young, productive, and smart and your child is full of raw potential that will one day blossom into world domination. Everywhere you and your child go, you encounter adoring strangers, because babies trigger a smile reflex that you don't need to be an anthropologist to understand. Humankind holds you in a warm embrace. And you smile knowingly when you encounter other parents with small children (all cute, since everyone is cute until the age of four) because you are part of a happy, healthy tribe and thrilled with the new reality you created just by having sex and buying a stroller.

This Mobius strip of parent–child wonder and perfection and genetic self-aggrandizement lasts until your child is nine. It is a sweet, wonderful period, but all too brief. And then the disappointment begins.

Parenthood, Phase 2: Your Child Disappoints You

My husband and I have always approached parenting differently, and the best analogy I can come up with is this: Having a child is like planting a tree. You put it in good soil and provide the water and sunlight required for optimal growth. Then, if you are my husband, you stand back to watch the tree grow, marveling when it has good seasons and worrying when it doesn't. If you are me, though, you pitch a tent next to the tree. You research the best fertilizers and hire arborists and whisper to the tree when no one is around. Ever vigilant, you chase away squirrels and mice and birds that look like they have bad intentions. From time to time, you apply insecticide. And you prune that tree. Constantly. Because without carefully shaping, God only knows what might happen to your tree. Things could get very, very out of control.

What can I say? It's the way I was raised. I remember having a conversation with my mother when I was in my late twenties and frustrated that my parents were still trying to manage many of my decisions. "Sweetheart," Mom explained, "it's really hard when you have a child and from the time they are born, you're sure you know what's right for them. Even when they are grown up, it's hard to know when to stop." You and your child were one, but as he grows, he separates from you, and that's painful. Plus, you probably do know what's right for your little homunculus. So you (try to) limit junk food and (try to) enforce bedtime routines and sign your kid up for one activity after another, looking for little glimmers of unusual talent like you're searching for pieces of sea glass on a crowded summer beach. And the disappointment creeps in.

Travel soccer, it turns out, is not going to lead to a Division 1 program.

Weekly cello lessons are not going to lead to Juilliard.

Math Olympiad is not going to lead to MIT.

The high-school newspaper will not lead to the *New York Times.*

An impromptu letter to Bill Gates is just a piece of fan mail he will never read.

As your child becomes more and more, well, average, you begin to regard the other members of your parenting tribe with suspicion. Do they know things you don't? Why can her kid name all the state capitals? How come he puts his dishes in your dishwasher without being asked? When did he learn to dribble like that? In other words, what are you doing wrong?

Self-doubt is a useful corrective, but it's tricky when it comes to parenting. If you are a thoughtful, responsible, hardworking person, you routinely question whether you are doing an optimal job raising your kids. The moments of questioning arrive without warning, such as when you hear about a kid in town who can speak multiple languages even though he's just starting seventh grade, which was what happened to me the other day. My youngest son, Axel, and I were on a bike ride and as we passed an ordinary-looking middle-school boy with a mouthful of braces and hair that looked like it needed cutting, Axel casually said, "Mom, see that kid? He can speak four languages."

"Oh?" I said, intrigued and already disturbed. "Which languages?"

"Spanish, French, Italian, and American," Axel said.

Two thoughts immediately popped into my head. First: *Once you know Spanish, it's not so hard to learn French and Italian, so big whoop, kid.* And second: *Does Axel, who is twelve years old, honestly think* AMERICAN *is a language?*

Obviously my son's offhand comment sent me spinning into several hours of punishing self-examination as I considered all the ways I have failed to help him develop into a genius, linguistic or otherwise. Too much screen time, for one, because excessive screen

time is to blame for every ill and inadequacy that be-
falls a modern child. I can't tell you exactly why screen
time is bad, but apparently it has something to do
with fresh air and imagination and the ability to read
facial expressions and problem-solve in the real world.
If your child has too much screen time, he will grow
up (or not grow up, as it were) into a person who lives
in your basement and plays Fortnite until three a.m.
Unless, of course, he grows up to be like Ninja, the
best, most famous Fortnite player in the world, who
allegedly makes five hundred thousand dollars a month
playing the game and whose success is invoked every
time I try to convince Axel that playing video games
will get him nowhere in life.

So too much screen time is probably the reason
Axel doesn't speak Italian. It could also be his diet, his
failure to meditate, his pre-teen aversion to hard work,
his sporadic sense of discipline, or his desire to watch
the movie *Ratatouille* for the twentieth time instead of
doing just about anything else.

Or it could be parental indifference. Axel is our
youngest child, and, as everyone knows, the vector of
parental energy and drive moves steadily toward a place
of lazy exhaustion with each addition to the family—let's
just say it's amazing the boy ever learned to use a fork.
After parental indifference takes hold, it's impossible to

get rid of, like black mold in the caulking around the bathtub. And the more it spreads, the greater the opportunity for the kids to do something disappointing.

Do you let kids drink alcohol at your house? Of course you don't! Not only is that illegal if they are under the age of twenty-one, but it's stupid, irresponsible, and opens you up to a whole world of liability. Naturally I would never, ever, *ever* do that. Until the time I did. We live in a small town, 2.4 square miles in total, most of it lined with sidewalks. Kids walk everywhere, and on mild nights you see packs of them wandering around, trying to avoid detection, scattering like cockroaches if you get too close. Unlike in my hometown, where after getting drunk at a friend's house, you had to drive home on winding country roads—yes, I'm lucky to be alive—in my kids' hometown, drinking and driving is just not something that's done (thanks to sidewalks and Uber). And thank God for that.

But there is a conundrum. When (and that's when, not if) your nineteen-year-old child drinks, would you prefer he do it somewhere beyond your view so you won't be informed until he's facedown on a stranger's lawn with EMS on its way? Or at your house with his friends, where you can semi-manage the situation and just pray you don't get sued?

Sometimes parental indifference provides the answer,

like the night our middle son, Hugo, then a college freshman, invited a bunch of friends over to play beer pong in our garage. He had asked my permission in the afternoon in a conversation that went like this:

"Mom, where's that folding table we used for my graduation party?"

"I don't know. Why?"

"We need it for beer pong."

"Nobody else has a table?"

"I don't think so."

"What, you're going to put it in the car? Where are you all going?"

"I don't know."

An hour later: "Mom, I found the table. It was in the basement."

"Whose house are you going to?"

"Well...I was wondering if we could play in the garage."

"Um. I don't know. I don't love that idea."

"I understand."

An hour later: "Mom, so can we play in the garage?"

"There's no other house where you can play?"

"No."

"Ugh. I don't know. Let me ask Dad."

An hour later: "Mom, I promise we'll be quiet. You won't even know we're there. And I'll clean up."

"Oh God, Hugo, I don't know. This is not a good idea."

And so it went. My nonanswer was the only answer Hugo needed, and before I knew it, it was ten p.m. and there were six nineteen-year-old boys with a stack of red Solo cups and two twelve-packs of beer in my garage. The next morning I got up to discover that someone had neatly chopped off the bulbous lavender head of each allium plant that had been blooming in my garden. I wasn't mad about the beer pong, but I was mad about the allium. Which just shows you what a lax, morally deficient, shitty mother I am.

To be clear: Parental indifference and the absence of parental worry are not the same thing, which you learn when your child turns twenty-one, no longer has to play beer pong in the garage, and can legally go to bars. It's true that when he is away at school, you have no idea what the hell he is doing, when—or if—he goes to bed, or how drunk or stoned he is when his head hits the pillow. Which is an arrangement that suits everyone. But when a child comes home from college, for holidays or for the summer, once again you feel the need to know where he is at all times. You remember how much fun it was to drink too much when you were his age, how everything was a fantastic joke, how a hangover didn't matter because a hangover meant you had such good stories to tell. But you *definitely* are not comfortable with your child having that kind of fun.

The other night, Hugo went into Manhattan on the train with a bunch of people he's known since middle school. Their whereabouts were a mystery and I'm not quite so helicopter-y that I would employ Find My Phone to figure it out, although I could have. All I know is that I woke up at 2:12 a.m. and Hugo's bed was empty; I woke up again at 4:25, and he still wasn't home. Don't bars in New York close at 2:00, or am I thinking of the last century? The sky was getting light and my mind went to the worst places, as minds tend to do when dawn is breaking and a child is unaccounted for. Hugo could have been at an all-night tattoo parlor or he could have been floating in the East River. I got out of bed, went downstairs to the kitchen, and called him.

He picked up on the first ring. "Hi, Mom," he said. "I'm in an Uber."

"Are you almost home?"

"I'll be there soon." Loud music was playing in the background, music that suggested *after-hours club* rather than *interior of a car*. "I'm sorry," he said, and I knew he meant it. He does not like me to worry even as he does things to cause it. "Late night." He added that the Uber was taking him to a friend's house, so

I could "just go back to sleep." This may have been thoughtfulness on his part or it may have been self-preservation, because the last time he came home from the city late he smelled like a distillery and we had to talk about that. But anyway, "just go back to sleep"— as if! I did experience a small moment of triumph the following afternoon when, hair standing on end and smelling only faintly of a distillery, Hugo said to me, "Mom, coming home at seven a.m. and seeing people out jogging and walking their dogs was one of the most depressing experiences of my entire life."

In phase 2 of parenting, when your child does something amazing, it's often not brilliant-amazing; it's amazing because of its cluelessness, recklessness, or rank stupidity. Now when you ask yourself, *Where did that come from?*, the answer is *Definitely not from me*. (I once stood in line at a Manhattan coffee shop in front of two middle-aged women and heard one say to the other, "If I can just keep him alive and out of jail until he's twenty-five, then I've done my job.")

After your child becomes a young adult—if that's what we can call a person who is old enough to drink alcohol, buy a vape pen, and enlist in the army but still needs help writing a proper e-mail and reminding that those dirty dishes in the sink don't wash themselves— your relationship shifts in ways that may be apparent only to you. Your kids see you as they always have: as a provider, an object of light scorn, a person who doesn't know who Childish Gambino is and who can't ask for anything without nagging. But you regard them differently, which creates tension. There is a gap in understanding; the roles all of you are playing have changed, but the director has told only half the cast.

It would be easier to be furious with your young-adult children if you didn't also pity them. They are so smart and so dumb, these kids. A friend of mine was stunned one day when her twenty-something daughter asked her, "What's a stamp?" I know this girl, and she is no idiot. Perhaps when you have grown up in the age of e-mail, U.S. Postal Service stamps are just not part of your reality. Still! *What's a STAMP?* My kids can use a 3-D printer but they don't really know how to mail a letter or leave a voice mail. Or, frankly, call someone on the phone. Owen was once invited to a bar mitzvah for a boy he didn't know very well, thrown by parents he knew even less and who had the effrontery to require that guests RSVP by phone. Owen was thirteen years old and, in my opinion, more than capable of calling to RSVP. But the thought of picking up the phone and dialing the number of an adult he didn't really know—and who might actually pick up!—was so overwhelming that he kept putting it off. The host mother was forced to leave a message on our answering machine five days before the party, asking whether Owen would attend. (There are a number of common-decency-type lessons American elementary schools would be wise to teach, and how to RSVP properly and promptly is one of them. How to let people off the elevator before you charge your way in is another.) Owen finally did call the mother, and it was a very short conversation, and then he had to go play on the computer for an hour and a half to recover.

Parenthood, Phase 3: Your Child Makes You Disappointed in Yourself

But your children continue to grow, both physically and in their understanding of the world and their place in it, and your life gets a lot more confusing. Their behavior becomes moderate and sensible, and your moments of frustration diminish accordingly. And then your disappointment turns inward, and the sadness creeps in with it. It's like bees, the sadness, carpenter bees that you have been watching with only mild interest until you see that they are actually boring holes in the wood siding of your house. There are grains of sawdust in telling little piles, and suddenly you begin to worry that the house is about to fall down. How did you let *that* happen?

But first, let's talk about the ridiculous, such as the fact that I have no idea which buttons to push on the remote. The other night I was tucking Axel in bed and started tickling him—teasing him in a good-natured way—and as a comeback, he shouted at me, through strangled laughter, "You don't even know how to turn on the TV!"

Oh, it's pathetic. If I want to watch something, I'm forced to rely on a child or a husband because we have one remote that is for the cable and another that is for the TV and one of the remotes can get Netflix and one turns up the volume and one or both actually change the channel. But with all the things I have to know in life, I'm sure as hell not going to prioritize *that* information in my brain.

It's karma's cruel joke that I spent my teenage years making fun of my father because he didn't know how to operate the VCR. How could a person be so inept? Now my own children reach over my shoulder and grab the mouse as I sit at the computer in the kitchen yelling at Steve Jobs because none of the products he made us addicted to includes an instruction booklet. Who's laughing now? Karma, that's who. Karma and Steve Jobs. The upside is that, the more confusing technology becomes, the more comfortable I am with death. Because when I'm dead, it won't matter that I can't turn on the TV.

At this age, in this third phase of parenting, inevitable as sunset, I am disappointed in myself. According to my children—and I can't help but agree—I am incompetent because I can't turn on the TV. But I know something else, which is that I'm also an inferior human being. Unlike their mother, my children don't gossip. They're not judgmental; they don't care about material things; they don't hold grudges. They don't get angry at the dogs for shedding or feel semi-martyred because no one else in the household does as much as they do. If you choose to pull out your phone at the dinner table, they don't boil over with rage. They give people the benefit of the doubt, which might be due to lack of experience with con artists and cranks, or it could be because they are superior humans. They know why the iCloud storage is full. They know why the app isn't working. They understand what TFW means on Instagram and will explain it to you, patiently. Good-humored, generous, and tolerant, they live in a world where boys can be born as girls and girls can be born as boys and a gay man can run for president and it's all just a giant *Who cares.*

This is the generation of people you and I brought

into the world, and they have taught us valuable lessons just by growing up. They have proven that comparing them to their peers is not helpful for anyone, and it's disappointing that you were so slow to understand that. The kid who spoke four languages in seventh grade has maybe gone on to get a PhD in linguistics or maybe works for Google or maybe lives in his parents' basement playing Fortnite until three a.m. The future of that kid does not matter to you and has nothing whatsoever to do with your own children. It turns out that the vector of parental energy and drive was headed not to a place of indifference but to one of acceptance. You see the flaws in your children but you don't try to change them, because once they reach young adulthood, they are responsible for their own flaw maintenance. Now when your child does something amazing, you once again ask yourself, *Where did that come from?* And the answer is *Who knows?* Because you realize it doesn't matter. Which is incredibly freeing.

It's disappointing that it took you two decades of parenting to get to this point of acceptance. And then there is the sadness, which is a disappointment all its own. Your kids have become well-adjusted young adults on their way to lives full of wonder and surprise, heartbreak and triumph. You should feel proud, and satisfied. So why are there days when you allow sadness for him to hold your hand in public. He hates school, he announces emphatically, because all kids say they hate school when they are twelve; to admit otherwise would be social suicide. Your older children are gone, perhaps, or if they are in high school, they are probably unbearable. Better not tangle with them unless it's absolutely necessary. You gaze wistfully at houses inhabited by families with elementary-school children, booster seats in the cars, swing sets in the yards, and you feel old and so envious, even though elementary school is clearly less fun now that, like dodgeball before it, birthday cupcakes have been banned, which you know because you read all those e-mails.

And so there is a heaviness. You think back to the days when everyone was younger—well, mostly you—and hope and excitement were freely and unselfconsciously expressed. You don't want to look forward, because forward just leads to an empty house, bad knees, and no one to help you turn on the TV.

Every time I get on the internet, I'm confronted with another article about how middle-aged women are so *terrific* now. We're strong and vital and running CBS News and General Motors and Denmark, and, by the way, fuck menopause. Who cares about menopause? It's natural and normal and we're all going to own it.

But I'm not letting go of sad. Because if I'm supposed to be optimistic and invincible all the time, then I'm unprepared when certain annual rituals, like the beginning of the school year, make me melancholy. Even if your children are happy and healthy, even while you're counting your blessings, sometimes the sadness prevails. I look at the face of one of my adult sons, searching his features for the boy he used to be. Every once in a while I get a little glimpse, a sparkle in the eyes or a tilt of the head, and it's like a portal has opened, just for a microsecond. In that moment I can make the connection; I can see the beginnings of this story. I understand how we all got to this moment, step by step. But then the portal door slams shut, and once again there is a man before me. Even though I have an intimate understanding of each child that began before he was born, there's so much I don't know about this person I pushed into the world. I wish I could have five more years, a dozen, a hundred. Is that how long it would take for me to fully understand him?

When I am waiting for one of my older sons to come home for a visit, I am like something out of a Victorian novel, a silent woman with a bursting heart. I stand watch at the front windows, looking for a car turning into the driveway; before my son has even touched the knob, I've opened the front door and flung myself at him.

It doesn't take long for the enthusiasm to wane. In a matter of hours after either of my older children comes home, there are five pairs of size 12 shoes scattered willy-nilly across the threshold. The conditioner disappears from my shower and there's a banana peel in the cupholder in the car. My recycling overflows with cans of Natural Light, like some sort of speed-growing fungus. Every day I have a conversation about whether it's my responsibility to Venmo money to my child for groceries, for gas, for a haircut, because the lines separating who should pay for what are extremely fuzzy. The music is too loud and the refrigerator is too full and there is always someone else's laundry in the machine when I want to do a load.

Then, before I know it, he's left again. And I am bereft. I once heard a woman describe her children this way: "They are my everything, everywhere, all the time." So what does she do when they leave?

Living in a house that is no longer filled with children is like finally receiving a box that contains the present you've wanted for years, only the box is empty. When there are children around, there is always something for you to do: Answer a question, prepare a lunch, apply a Band-Aid, settle a dispute. Set a limit, teach a skill, course-correct, comfort. And then one day you find yourself in the kitchen on a Saturday morning and no one needs you. The hours stretch out before you and you don't know how you're going to fill them. This new reality is liberating, to be sure. This is what you've been waiting for! So why do you feel lost?

As I type this sentence, I am completely alone at home, which in this phase of my life happens only once or twice a year. I'm sitting on my front porch and the sun has set, but the sky is still light in a way that calls to mind René Magritte's Empire of Light series, paintings I have always loved. Hugo has gone back to college and Owen is out of town, and Axel and my husband are playing tennis. Even the dogs are gone. It's 7:47 p.m. and I'm listening to the crickets and the front door is wide open, since the dogs are away with Owen so I don't have to worry that any second, one of them is going to sprint out to the street and, as I watch, get run over by a car, which happened to our collie Peabody when I was in fourth grade and which I have never gotten over. The night is beautiful and I am all alone with no one to provide for, supervise, respond to, feed, or acknowledge. A feeling of serenity and goodwill has washed over me and I swear it has nothing to do with the glass of wine that's within arm's reach. No. I have just realized this is what it feels like to be truly . . . relaxed. And it's intoxicating. (Again, *not the wine*.) I notice the crickets and the green-black silhouette of the trees against the light sky and I feel centered and peaceful and happy. Even if I know that I wouldn't want this to last forever. My time alone on the porch is magic precisely because it's occasional, and brief, and stolen.

I'm not ready for the gift of a house that is child-free. Call it denial or call it fear, but I'm not ready for my kids to leave me. The reason most of us had children in the first place was not because of a narcissistic need to spread our genetic material throughout the world. The decision to have children was born out of love. Maybe the origin story is no longer relevant; maybe that particular love is damaged, or gone. But something else has grown from it—a complicated, annoying miracle of a person with a story you hope lasts a lot longer than your own. When you allow yourself to overlook how your children frustrate you, how they disappoint you and make you disappointed in yourself, you can see them for what they are: fellow travelers trying to make their way with purpose through an enormous world. And you are better off if you stick together.

Owen recently completed a teaching job that lasted two years. It was fulfilling but exhausting, and overwhelming for a kid just out of college. Now he's trying to figure out what to do next. The other night he picked me up at the train station and I asked how he spent his day.

Chapter 5

How I Learned to Stop Worrying and Love the Roomba

There is a unique kind of middle-age, modern-era rage that erupts when you call your credit-card company because you don't recognize a charge on your bill. Maybe it's true that your spouse made the charge, but the fact that your spouse wasn't listening when you asked about it is not the reason for the rage. The rage— and it's not anger or frustration; it's rage—comes when you have to have a "conversation" with a machine or press four hundred and sixty-five buttons on your phone in order to reach a real human. You've tried to maintain your equanimity as, with each passing day, technology advances further beyond your understanding. Still, there is something about talking to a machine that has replaced a person that is simply . . . enraging.

Unless that machine is my vacuum robot, aka Roomba. I can talk to my Roomba all day. Our conversations, while short, are always meaningful. For example, I might tell Roomba that it's the best thing that has ever happened to me, and Roomba will reply, "Error eighteen, please open the iRobot app for help."

Now that automation has taken so many tedious items off humanity's collective to-do list, I suppose I should be angry and scared about robots that can do my job. As time marches on, however, I become a lazier human being, and so I am very, very grateful for the cute little round guy with the Gatsby-esque green light who knows not to vacuum over the towel my son dropped on the floor the day before yesterday.

Our world is moving on autopilot, and the sooner you come to grips with that, the sooner you can get comfortable with the fact that Alexa will one day be your boss. I read once that researchers at the University of Oxford had analyzed 702 occupations in the United States and determined that half of them are at high risk of being automated in the next couple of decades. (Realtors, accountants, telemarketers: Don't panic, but have you considered, say, education or dentistry?) Apparently, McKinsey and Company conducted research that showed that certain professions are headed for a future of nearly 100 percent automation. I'm just waiting for "wife and mother" to appear on that McKinsey list, because I've got a bag packed and am ready to hop in my driverless car and hit the road. I'm not sure where I'll eventually end up, just someplace where my family will never find me.

In the meantime, I will continue to explore my relationship with Roomba. What began as an experiment in domestic codependent coexistence between woman and robot has turned into something that resembles love. It's not just me. I once worked with a woman who was having a secret affair with her Roomba. Every morning while her husband was taking the kids to school, she would remove Roomba from the box, let Roomba clean her apartment floor, then put Roomba back in the box before her husband returned. I never got to the bottom of why she did this, and while I pretended to find her story vaguely disturbing, let's just say there's a reason I made her tell it to me so many times.

I also read recently that researchers at institutions

of higher learning are developing robots that can de-cipher human emotion. When I am replaced by a wife/mother robot in my own household, I'm taking my suitcase straight up to Boston to ask the folks at MIT exactly why I fell in love with Roomba. There are other bigger, fancier domestic robots that seem to deliver more, like the smart refrigerator with a door that turns transparent when you touch it and that can also provide a weather report and order products from Amazon Prime. But I don't need a refrigerator to buy stuff for me. Call me when it can make veal Marsala.

Until the researchers at MIT have it figured out, I will just have to guess at the logic behind my devotion to Roomba. Maybe I've done so much vacuuming in my life that I'm happy to be replaced. Maybe it was the video I saw online of the Roomba that whirred its way around Gauge the puppy lying on the kitchen floor, which I have now watched about twelve times. Or maybe it's the way Roomba sometimes goes around and around in circles with no clear purpose, looking directionless and confused but always getting the job done in the end. Just like a middle-aged human.

Chapter 6

The Shalom Ambulette, or How to Know If Your Career Is Over

A few weeks after I became unemployed, my youngest son asked me to take an online quiz. Axel was in fourth grade and had a new interest in Greek mythology. The quiz was called "Which Greek God Are You?"

I don't remember the questions, but I remember the answer: I was Hera, the wife and sister of Zeus, who uses his power to win her and then screw her over time and again. She's the protector of women and children, but she's also super-angry and super-vengeful. She's a badass with a really mean streak, but her heart is more or less in the right place.

I almost laughed out loud when I saw the quiz result. It made perfect sense. After decades of a successful career I was suddenly, for the first time in my life, a stay-at-home mom. But I felt spiteful and burned with a vengeful wish to see the morons who had destroyed my professional world turned into bears, set upon by snakes, or chased by gadflies to a distant part of the world.

• • •

A thoughtful man I know said we all need to ask ourselves these three questions:

1. Who am I?
2. Where am I going?
3. Why am I going there?

Once you are past thirty, you probably know the answer to the first question. Once you reach forty, you have answered the second. And once you are in your fifties, as I am now, you'll ask yourself the third question often, and if you don't like the answer, you have to quit your job.

I know very few women my age who are satisfied with their careers, even if they survived the economic collapse of the coronavirus pandemic. Many of us were satisfied—or at least satisfied-ish—in our forties, when things were good enough and we were busy trying to figure out how to answer work e-mails and make school lunches at the same time. Your fifties, however, is the decade of "Wait, is this really it?" There is this little thing called meaning, and suddenly you want your days to be filled with it. Because there's only so much time.

During the course of my twenty-five-year magazine career, I frequently encountered young women (they were always women) who wanted to know how I had engineered my life. They were college students or recent graduates, seasoned internship-getters, their faces shining with fervor and intention. I always felt like a bit of a fraud giving advice to these young women, all of them A students who expected, with the right kind of planning, to keep getting As for the rest of their lives. In all honesty, my start in magazines felt like an accident; it was like I was walking down the middle of the street in Manhattan and someone had left a manhole cover off and I fell into the hole and suddenly I was sitting in Anna Wintour's *Vogue* office, wearing a red rayon dress with white polka dots that I had bought at the Ann Taylor outlet and that I believed was sufficiently stylish. That's how much planning (and fashion understanding) went into the beginnings of my professional life.

Until the age of twenty-seven I existed in what I now think of as a state of general confusion in which I was optimistic, energetic, curious, and clueless. I was a good student, but I had no idea where being smart, hard-working, conscientious, and good at passing notes to boys would take me later in life. I was not the president of anything. I did not spend a summer building houses in Guatemala, and I did not cold-call strangers for informational interviews. When I thought about my future, which wasn't often, I imagined I would be a stay-at-home mom, because I had had a happy childhood and that's how my own mom spent most of my early life.

I read constantly when I was young. Every week in the summer, I checked out as many books as the public library allowed and plowed through them on the screened porch, a bowl of cherries in my lap. And I was writing, writing just for fun, writing with what my friend Jim calls "no attachment to outcome," which is an easy way to approach just about anything when you are fourteen. This was before e-mail; I would go to my father's big wooden desk, take one of his long yellow legal pads, and write letters. For one whole summer I wrote exclusively to my high-school best friend, Ann Bardsley, who lived all of twenty miles away. We both pretended to be characters from *The Age of Innocence*. At that time, living in small-town

Delaware with no attachment to outcome, I was happy to let Edith Wharton teach me everything I thought I needed to know about New York City.

I started working for money when I was fifteen, cleaning my father's law office. I worked at Happy Harry's drugstore; at the local Westvaco paper factory; at a U.S. Senate office; for a creepy photographer; for a successful artist of limited talent; in a bookstore; as a temporary secretary in a big Philadelphia law firm; in the office of Columbia University's General Studies department; and for a commercial film production company that was slowly going out of business. And then *Vogue,* and the discovery phase of my life. In landing there—not at *Vogue,* per se, but at a magazine—I found my place and my people. I was eager and confident, and that feeling lasted nearly twenty years.

Things weren't easy at the beginning of the *Vogue* job. I had a fairly useless graduate degree and was answering phones and getting coffee for editors who were essentially my age. But there was a Stockholm syndrome thing that happened at *Vogue,* and it trickled down to the assistants. Anna Wintour was She, and we all spent a lot of time wondering what She was thinking or what She meant when she scribbled *See me* in a heavy, furious hand across a manuscript that one of her assistants hurried back to its editor. She reminded me of a praying mantis, the insect I fear most: impossibly thin and mostly silent, mysterious and all-powerful and spectacular in nearly every way. Most days, my fellow assistants and I would walk up Madison Avenue to Mangia on Forty-Eighth Street to get sandwiches for lunch, and even now, all these years later, I recall precisely how the basil parmesan chicken salad tasted. It was perfect, and not just because I was able to pay for it out of petty cash, that magic drawer that provided an endless supply of free coffee, free taxis, free lunch. (One fashion editor was said to have furnished her entire Hamptons house with furniture and props from her shoots, so everyone on staff referred to her house, with a mixture of derision and awe, as Petty Cash Junction.)

Eventually I was promoted at *Vogue,* and I didn't have to answer anyone's phone ever again. I got pregnant with Owen, which presented a clothing challenge, because without a trust fund or VIP access to the best sample sales, I had a hard enough time dressing well even without being pregnant. Throughout my pregnancy, whenever I walked into Anna's office, finding her as always perched on the edge of her hard-backed metal chair, she would regard my midsection with a look that seemed to me to say, *Ugh . . . it's still there?* Wearing lots of black on black seemed to be the answer. One week during my pregnancy I reported for jury duty in Brooklyn and a fellow juror, a kindly older woman, pulled me aside, squeezed both my forearms, and said, "You are in such a joyful time of your life. You should be wearing color, not black!" I smiled and agreed with her but thought to myself, *Lady, you have no idea.*

After I had Owen, Anna sent me an engraved sterling-silver baby cup from Tiffany, an act of generosity and thoughtfulness that just added to her scary, praying mantis mystique.

In my daily life—editing the horoscope by Athena Starwoman (yes, really), fine-tuning captions about the big three (Christy Turlington, Naomi Campbell, Linda Evangelista), marching up to Mangia in last season's Gucci stilettos that I bought at the Woodbury Common outlet mall—did I feel like I had a purpose? Oh, who cared! I had a job, a job that looked like it could turn into a career, and it was fun!

After Owen was born, I left *Vogue* for *Premiere,* which had a less wonderful office space and a more wonderful boss, Susan Lyne, who gave me a nice bump up from my *Vogue* salary. Unlike Anna, who traveled by car service, Susan—who was tall and blond, a former hippie who lived on the Upper East Side—took the subway to work. But she flew business class when she went to LA, and I got to fly business class when I went to LA too. *Premiere* was scrappy, staffed by journalists who cared about the art of filmmaking first and the lives of movie stars a distant second.

I was so happy. I was young and healthy and full of hope with a beautiful baby boy, a loving husband, a terrific two-bedroom rental in Brooklyn, and a fat tabby cat named George who could fetch like a dog and who escaped through the window when our apartment was broken into but returned the following day, because that was exactly the kind of luck I had back then.

After *Premiere* was sold to a new owner, Susan Lyne quit. She parlayed her Hollywood journalism experience into a big job at Disney. I should have watched Susan more closely. There were women in the magazine world who could see the future, take their experiences and contacts, stir them in a big pot, and come out with a big beautiful bowl of new-job-in-new-industry. I would come to realize that not everyone had that talent.

After Susan left, the magazine went through two new editors in chief in quick succession and I began to meet my husband during lunch and on street corners to cry about my job, which meant it was time for a new one. From *Premiere* I went to *Travel + Leisure* (nice + boring), back to *Vogue* (better job + Stockholm syndrome), and then to *Glamour,* where I was hired by Bonnie Fuller, a genius Canadian who wore dresses like sausage casings and who struck me as the idiot savant of the New York magazine world. When Bonnie left, she was replaced by Cindi Leive, a friend of mine since the college summer when we both took the Bennington College writers workshop, where we smoked cigarettes and pretended not to stare at Bret Easton Ellis, who was just our age but who had catapulted into another stratosphere with the recent publication of his first novel, *Less Than Zero*.

Then I got a call from Time Inc. about the editor in chief job at a three-year-old magazine called *Real Simple*. Unlike every other place I had worked, *Real Simple* spoke to me as a reader—a busy working mother who was just trying to find a manageable level of control in her daily life. The photographs and design were so calming, they were like meditation, or Xanax. Plus, none of the cover lines exhorted you to buy designer shoes or improve your sex life.

But how to be a boss? I spent many hours worrying about this. Anna was a cipher and Susan was breezy and Bonnie was robotic and Cindi was indefatigable and Kristin was...what? Was Kristin stern and distant or warm and chummy? Did Kristin keep her staff at arm's length or try to be one of them? There was no guidebook. What if I got it wrong? Finally my husband said, "They hired you for who you are. Just be yourself, and that will be fine."

And it was. It was more than fine—much more.

There is something almost miraculous about having a job in which the skills you possess completely match up with the requirements of the work. It was as if each thing I had done up to that point—from factory to Capitol Hill, graduate school to commercial film production—was one thin piece of a multilayered, intricate lock, and when I landed at *Real Simple* all of the elements aligned with a soft click and everything suddenly sprung open. And inside was . . . magic.

• • •

The summer before I started fifth grade, I entered a 4-H cooking contest at the state fair in Harrington, Delaware. It was my mother's idea. I wore a plaid cotton skirt and a white short-sleeved T-shirt with a picture of a girl holding a flower. The day was extremely hot, and my hair, held back with a side barrette to keep it out of the way while I cooked for the judges, stuck to my temples with sweat. Along with the judges, my mother watched silently, nervously, as I prepared Tuna Chinese Cashew Casserole from her recipe, sprinkled crunchy noodles on top, and set exactly one place, using as decorative flair a bamboo place mat and a pair of chopsticks, about the only "Asian" things I could get my hands on. My mother thought I'd torpedoed my chances when I licked my finger in front of the judges after opening the can of Campbell's Cream of Mushroom soup that the recipe required, but somehow I prevailed and won a blue ribbon. My picture even appeared in the newspaper: I stood in front of my winning place setting, not smiling even though I felt like it, because the older girl beside me hadn't smiled when her photograph was taken.

How could I have known that the Delaware state fair would prepare me for corporate life? My childhood was spent at the knee of my patient, extremely competent mother, a former high-school head cheerleader and college home economics major who raised three girls to run their own households as enthusiastically and smoothly as she ran hers. Overseeing the editorial staff at *Real Simple* enabled—required—me to use what I knew about making a birthday cake from scratch and sewing on a button and planting a perennial and housebreaking a dog: the soft domestic skills I learned from the time I could tie my own shoes. The fact that I knew how to iron a shirt was not something I ever would have put on a résumé or mentioned in an interview ("And the strip of fabric that holds the buttons is actually called the *placket!*"), but this job was different. As a *Glamour* colleague put it, "*Real Simple* is a magazine for women whose mothers never taught them all that stuff." Suddenly I was Betty Crocker with a nineteen-million-dollar budget, a staff of seventy, and a corner office at Fiftieth and Sixth.

Thus began my decade of bliss. I doubled the circulation of the magazine, launched TV shows and product lines, published books and international issues, developed social-media channels and apps. I won a bunch of awards, hired a bunch of people, and grew *Real Simple* into the second-biggest brand in all of Time Inc. Along the way I became one of the longest-serving editors in the history of the company, which perhaps meant I was a survivor and perhaps meant I was a chump.

And the resources! When I got to Time Inc., the halls might as well have been wallpapered with hundred-dollar bills. You heard stories; my favorite was the one about the publisher who, under orders from his wife, used to take the drapes from his house with him on business trips so he could send them to the hotel dry cleaner and have the company pay for it. There was money everywhere, pouring in from happy readers all over the country and flying out the door like a magic carpet for those of us lucky enough to take the ride. For a decade, *Real Simple* was the darling of the magazine world and I was the darling of Time Inc., arguably the most historically important, pedigreed magazine company in the world, a company founded on solid journalistic principles with products designed for and produced by intelligent grown-ups who valued brains over beauty.

By the time I got there, Time Inc. was part of the Time Warner family, and when the company had its yearly internal awards ceremony, corporate communications would seat me next to the CEO because my magazine was growing and valuable and because I knew how to make small talk that conveyed that I was smart and important but knew the powerful man next to me was much smarter and much, much more important. What I didn't realize as I discussed a mutual acquaintance with Dick Parsons or taught Jeff Bewkes one of the few Dutch phrases that I knew (*Zit jij makkelijk,* or "You sit comfortably," which is what you say to a family member who won't help with the dinner dishes) was that I was in enemy territory.

Because what the Time Warner CEO knew that I didn't was that magazines were going the way of the Model T and the seltzer man and the player piano. Magazines as both cultural artifact and source of profit were in decline. When a legacy business is dying, there is no one moment that signals the beginning of the end, just as there is no discrete moment when youthful confidence ends and midlife identity crisis begins. But there is a feeling, and you know it's growing, even if you can't define it. You begin to suspect you're rearranging deck chairs on the *Titanic*. Magazine-making is a dynamic, collaborative, and, best of all, creative enterprise, but when Americans started reading everything on their phones instead of paying money at a newsstand, the bean counters took over. And when bean counters take over, they call in the management consultants, and then people like me begin to die just a little bit every day, like a plant someone mistakenly put in a south-facing window and then forgot to water.

Perhaps I would have grasped what was happening to my professional world if I had paid more attention to the signals. No doubt there were small, silent signs, like fruit flies in the kitchen that lead you to the rotting banana in the bowl on the counter. But I was busy running a sixty-five-million-dollar business and, more important, having a life. In that decade of bliss, I also:

- bought my dream house, a hundred-year-old shingled Victorian with turquoise kitchen walls, squirrels in the attic, knob-and-tube wiring, and bathroom pipes that froze if you didn't keep the water running on cold nights;
- spent a lot of money renovating the dream house; and
- had another baby, because why not?

There was so much excitement and growth in my home life that I didn't notice my professional lights beginning to dim. Then, in the spring of 2013, Sheryl Sandberg published *Lean In*. And although it was meant to be a motivational rallying cry, *Lean In* just made me...tired. Perhaps I was just too old to hear Sandberg's message; I had made the professional uphill climb of my twenties and thirties and was now standing at the top. But suddenly I didn't like the view. I saw before me a lot of what I didn't want to be doing, and unfortunately, that meant much of my job. I was in my late forties and I was overwhelmed, tired, frustrated, bored. Most of all, I had stopped believing in what I was doing.

For about six months when he was a junior in college, my son Owen convinced himself that he wanted to start his career as a management consultant. He was a double major in the honors program at a prestigious state university and—effortlessly, it seemed to me—got a 4.0 just about every semester. He has always been an extremely reasonable kid, and he reasoned that management consulting would allow him to see inside all sorts of industries and companies and enable him to figure out what he really wanted to do with his life. Which may have been right, but whatever. I thought of all of the smarty-pants management consultants I had worked with over the years and pulled out every warning I could think of:

"You will never sleep."

"You will live out of hotel rooms."

"You will work your ass off."

"You will probably be really, really bored."

None of these warnings seemed to work. Then I thought of the moment in *Pride and Prejudice,* one of Owen's favorite books, after Mr. Collins proposes to Lizzy and her father tells her, "From this day you must be a stranger to one of your parents. Your mother will never see you again if you do *not* marry Mr. Collins, and I will never see you again if you *do*." And so I said to Owen, "Oh, honey, it's totally fine if you want to be a management consultant. Just know that I won't ever speak to you again." Maybe I can't take credit, but after Owen graduated from college with honors, he became a fourth-grade teacher.

• • •

Which management-consulting firm was I working with when I had that conversation with my son? McKinsey, Bain, Boston Consulting Group? That company from Colorado that no one had ever heard of? God knows. I'd lost track. But I was firing people, and it certainly wasn't my idea.

In my twenty-five-year magazine career, I got better at a number of things over time: running meetings, appearing on TV, understanding the three things most American women want (black pants that fit, new chicken recipes, a great face cream with SPF). But firing people became harder over time, and I think I got worse at it. Firing an employee for cause is, if not easy, at least doable, in part because you know the person brought it on herself. (I'm reminded of a desk plaque I saw once in a store in New York: I'LL BE NICER IF YOU'LL BE SMARTER.) And when you fire an employee for cause, that person is usually not surprised. You have warned her time and again that she needs to change, and yet somehow she can't or won't do it.

But when you begin firing employees simply be-cause some bullshit "efficiency" has been identified by a chirpy, overachieving consultant two years out of Wharton who has never picked up a magazine—well, those are the kinds of firings that leave you crying at your desk as soon as the shocked staffer who trusted you with her career and income walks out of your office and closes the door behind her. I was once a person who prized efficiency, who thought that, both as a concept and a way to conduct your life, *maximum efficiency* was a worthy goal. I didn't realize until the end of my magazine days that the management consultants had co-opted *efficiency* and turned it into something sinister.

It is hard to describe how much it sucks to hire a wonderful creative team, people you admire for their talent and love because they make your work-days so joyful, and then have to start firing them. A fellow editor likened the increasing rounds of firing to contractions—first you fire people every couple of years, then once a year, then every six months, and then each quarter before the earnings call. And what pops out in the end is not a new baby, not euphoria and magic, but an ugly facsimile of your magazine, full of factual errors and bad grammar and stock photographs supplied by some well-meaning but poorly trained colleague who works in Bangalore.

Yes, I was the *firer,* not the *fired*. All things considered, I was not entitled to complain. But years of dropping the guillotine take their toll. When I was in my late thirties and newish in the job, I used to, if not leap out of bed every morning, at least climb out with purpose and en-thusiasm. But once I hit the ten-year mark at *Real Simple* and the fifty-year mark at life, I had not only started to drag—I had become a drag. There was a dull heaviness to the way I moved through the world, griping about the faux difficulties in my privileged existence. I hated it.

Feet in the metal stirrups during my annual pelvic exam, I mused to my gynecologist: "I think I'm either going through perimenopause, suffering from depression, or need to find a new job." She looked up at me over the tent of my legs and said, "Or maybe it's all three."

Super!

Without intending to, I began to develop a list of questions that seemed, like a gentle hand on the small of my back, to direct me toward the door:

1. If every time someone on the executive team sends out a company-wide e-mail, my initial response is *BARF,* is that a problem?

2. If, while putting mascara on one morning, I tell my husband that "a big job working for executive morons is not how I define *success,*" am I getting too toxic and cranky to be a good partner?

3. If I get up in front of my magazine staff in full rah-rah mode and try to energize them to do good work but know I may have to fire a quarter of them within the next year, am I just a big fraud?

4. If I can't focus in meetings because I am too busy wondering whether I am going to have a glass of wine

or a beer when I get home, does that mean I am deeply, deeply bored?

5. If every time I have a budget meeting it feels like someone has said to me, *Okay, we are going to cut off seven of your toes and then you will show us how you are going to become a professional ballerina,* is it time to step aside?

6. If I am driving on the Hutchinson River Parkway one morning and see a little ambulance called Shalom Ambulette with a DRIVER WANTED sign taped to the back window, and, even though I don't speak Hebrew and have never driven anything for a living and don't even know the difference between an ambulance and an ambulette, I consider for a second whether I would like that job, is it time to make a change?

. . . and finally:

7. If I believe that the men above me in the company hierarchy are incompetent assholes and yet I stay in the job, does that mean I am failing both myself and something larger? Am I failing feminism?

That last question came one day as I watched the CEO of Time Inc.—a man I considered a sexist nincompoop—give a town-hall speech and wondered, not for the first time, whether it would make me happy to see him fall off the stage. Was I such a horrible person that I genuinely wanted this man to hurt and humiliate himself in front of two hundred people? Or was it an idle fantasy, like the fantasy that bloomed in my head the time I saw Julie Andrews in the security line at JFK airport, right in front of me? She was wearing leggings and a baseball cap and had that incredible Julie Andrews posture and I fantasized that she was going to turn to me and say, "You look like a very charming woman and you have excellent posture too and I'd love for you to sit next to me in first class all the way to California." I didn't really want to sit next to Julie Andrews on that flight. But it was a nice thought. As was the thought that my CEO could fall off the stage and hit his head hard enough that he would have to be hospitalized, if only for observation.

I didn't know it yet, but I had become Hera, filled with a bubbling, subcutaneous anger. In my experience, *angry* is not a great mindset when you need to lead a team of seventy people whose livelihoods depend on you putting out a cheery magazine that is supposed to inspire two million American women every month. Anger is distracting, and even if you get Botox to make the frown lines disappear, as I did, it turns out you can't Botox the

anger away. Eventually the anger spills out into everything in your life—you're angry at your husband for not
putting his clothes in the hamper and at your children
for walking through the living room with dirty cleats
and at your babysitter for putting the jelly in the pantry
instead of the refrigerator and at your dogs for their refusal to stop shedding and at your friends for daring to
want to have a drink with you on a Thursday night.

And this is very, very bad.

I've always admired rebels because I was never brave
enough to be one myself. I was an eldest-child line-
toer, someone who never took too many napkins at
fast-food restaurants and always remembered to recycle,
the daughter of a Dutch immigrant who believed that
roads should be straight and the garage kept as clean
as the kitchen. I did not break rules. I exercised, took
vitamins, turned off my phone at night—all the things
the *New York Times* health stories told me to do if I
wanted to live to be at least eighty-five without getting
type 2 diabetes or breaking a hip.

I toed the line at work too, head down, nose to the
grindstone, conforming to all the clichés about achiev-
ing the American dream. Even when my job got suckier,
even when I stopped being an editor and became a
person whose job it was to look for loose change under
the sofa cushions—even then I was a good girl. I was

not a rebel, because here's how a rebel would have behaved: Every time her tacky, ridiculous CEO bumped into her at a company function and, with a drink in his hand and a dress shirt stretched tight over his expansive abdomen, told her with disgust that her magazine spent as much money developing blueberry muffin recipes as *Time* magazine did in sending reporters to Iraq, a rebel would have replied, "That may be so, but those blueberry muffins make you a lot more money than those reporters do. So why don't you go fuck yourself?"

• • •

Our veterinarian once told my husband a story about a friend of his, another vet who used to treat large animals. This friend had sold his practice and given up his life's work because, as our vet explained to my husband, "He went one day to see a horse and woke up three months later in the hospital." The horse had kicked the veterinarian in the chest, causing cardiac arrest, and he had been in a coma for twelve weeks. That was it for him—no more large-animal work.

That's how leaving my job felt: like I was kicked in the chest by a horse in 2010, went into a coma, woke up six years later, and realized in a flash that it was all over.

The first domino tipped when my cell phone rang as

I stood in my kitchen at 7:09 on a weekday morning. The caller was a colleague I barely knew, phoning to inform me that he was my new boss. (Could he have told me that in person? Yes, but we're not going to dwell on that. Let's just say that managing up turned out to be his real strength.) A few days later my new boss told me about the next round of draconian cuts I would have to make to my budget. And so I was faced with a decision: Do I keep firing my staff, or do I fire myself? I made an appointment to see him. He sat across from me with his hands on his knees as I took a breath and then said, "I've spent the last thirteen years building this business. And now you are asking me to tear it apart."

"I'll call the head of HR," he said.

I nodded. By 5:30 that day, I had a severance agreement.

When I got on the train to go home, I made a list of things I would not miss about my job:

- high heels
- working out at 5:30 a.m. because that's when I had time
- people who talked in meetings just to talk
- my e-mail in-box
- sitting all day

- talking about millennials like they alone had the secret to the survival of the entire species
- trying to do more with less
- centralization
- Knoll office furniture
- having to swipe my ID card, Big Brother–style, to exit the building
- offices that were too cold in the summer and too hot in the winter
- waking up at 3:00 a.m. and worrying about personnel problems
- office carpeting
- firing people right before Christmas
- firing people right after they'd had a baby
- firing people in the spring, summer, fall, and winter
- firing people because there wasn't enough money
- firing people because someone else told me I had to

There were also things I knew I'd miss:

- making a product that was adored by countless people I will never meet
- my colleagues, except the ones I detested
- laughing at work
- corporate nonsense . . . when it was funny and didn't involve firing people

119

When it was time, I gathered the magazine staff in the conference room, the Hudson River sparkling out the window and my new boss sitting against the wall. I had written a little speech on my phone, which I'd tried to memorize before I went into the meeting. I stuck to the script for seven seconds and then burst into tears. I looked for Ann, my longtime assistant and my rock; she was sitting halfway down the long table. "Ann! Fuck!" I exclaimed, helpless. "I didn't want to cry."

Then my new boss stood up. "When I got this job," he began, "I met with the editors of every magazine in the company. I guess you could say it was kind of like speed-dating. We have a lot of talented editors here," he said, "but there was only one I wanted to take back to the honeymoon suite: Kristin."

Wait, what?

"Blah-blah-blah," he continued as I tried to process what he was saying, wondering what a honeymoon suite had to do with anything, wondering just how tone-deaf a grown man could be.

Oh, there were other indignities on the way out. Like the time the CEO, wearing a pastel golf shirt, walked past the glass-walled office in which I was saying goodbye to a former boss. He briefly made eye contact with me, then quickly looked away. (Note to

CEOs everywhere: The generous, appropriate thing to do in that situation is not to speed up on the way to the men's room but to pop your head in and say, "Heard you're leaving—we wish you all the best.")

Or the time an HR person said, "To be totally honest, it's not like you make such a big salary that the company will save much money in replacing you." (Note to HR people everywhere: This one should be filed under Top Ten Things Not to Say to a Longtime Employee When She Departs.)

Or the times, the many times, when people asked me, "What do you want to do?" I usually said, "Nothing," which was clearly an unacceptable answer, one that generated blank stares. (Note to fellow humans: In this situation, *nothing* could indeed mean "nothing." Or it could mean "I am having a midlife crisis and I don't know what to do so I am taking a dramatic step that might be completely wrong at this particular time or frankly at any time whatsoever but I am out of ideas please send help." The only appropriate response? "Sounds great!" Or, maybe, "Should I call someone?")

On the day I actually left, I went through the open-plan office, aisle by aisle, cubicle to cubicle. I called out, "Walk away now if you don't want me to hug you!" I was crying, naturally, but I wasn't the only one. People rose from their chairs and gave me a standing ovation. I cried harder. I was carrying flowers wrapped in brown paper and a few small boxes and the stuff that was too fragile to send home by UPS. Laden with packages, I made my way to the elevator, the staff of the magazine that I had loved so much trailing behind. It was both the most awkward and the most touching moment of my working life. And then the elevator doors closed, and the best job I'd ever had was over.

When I was in my thirties I had two miscarriages in quick succession. After the second one, my friend Donald, who is an artist, gave me a brightly painted box and a thick gray shoelace. He instructed me to put my sadness in the box and use the shoelace to tie it closed. When I took the elevator down from the ninth floor and walked out of that building for the last time, I put it all in a box: the happiness and satisfaction and pride, the disappointment and sadness and anger— everything that had provided my sense of self for so many years. I tied the box closed with the shoelace, and it stayed that way for a long time.

Chapter 7

Facebook? Check.
Twitter? Check.
Instagram? Check.
Snapchat? I Give Up

Back when I was a corporate citizen, I went to a conference and heard Evan Spiegel, the CEO of Snapchat who was, at the time, twenty-five years old, proclaim, "We've made it very hard for parents to embarrass their children." Immediately I understood why my two older boys spent 83 percent of their waking hours on that app with the little ghost icon that lets you send out a video of yourself doing something weird or marginally funny that disappears seconds after it's viewed. I am a mom and a social-media stalker, and the mere fact of my existence makes my children feel embarrassed. Until Snapchat, that is. Suddenly the tables were turned.

While I am well aware that technology makes my life much easier, I also just want to go live at *Downton Abbey* in season 1, before Lord Grantham installs the telephone. (Because you know how it goes: as soon as Lord Grantham installs the phone, widows have trysts with potential husbands in hotels and women start running London magazines and before long the dowager countess is addicted to Snapchat.) Alas, there is no returning to the days when I would be expected to wear a tiara to dinner, and so I must adapt. Meet my children where they live, as it were.

Here is my contract with my kids: *I pay for your phone, so I get to follow you on social media. I agree never to comment, like, share, or otherwise announce my presence in your digital life. And I will keep my opinions to myself. Until I can't.*

One morning when Hugo was a senior in high school, I was conducting "virtual oversight" of a class-mate he was suddenly spending a lot of time with but whom I had never met. I saw on the friend's Twitter profile a photo of my child doing something spectac-ularly stupid. I texted Hugo and said, *You should tell [what's-his-name] to remove that photo of you. Your guidance counselor can see that picture, and so can your teachers and college admissions people.* Oh, nervy mother! The gall of me, his parent, trying to protect him from his own impulsive, shortsighted, prefrontal-cortex–challenged teenage self! We went through the sadly familiar motions of an extended text fight (shouldn't there be a name for that? *Fexting*?) about boundaries, how I didn't respect them, he had no privacy, I ruined everything, I was so embarrassing, et cetera. But within hours the friend took the photo down. And, naturally, made all of his tweets private.

In the name of protective motherhood, I chase my children around social media like Alice in Wonderland down the rabbit hole. But every time I land someplace where the story starts to make sense, my kids change the narrative. As soon as I understood Facebook, they fled to Twitter. Once I got Twitter, they escaped to Instagram. To Luddites like me, each platform is a little less intuitive than the last. Now all anybody talks about is TikTok, and by the time you kindly read this essay, there will be a handful of new platforms to thrill teenagers and befuddle parents the world over.

As my children know, Snapchat is the one that broke me. It was just like the Cheshire Cat—there but not there. After I attended the conference and listened to Evan Spiegel (looked like he was about twelve, flew helicopters for fun; curiouser and curiouser!), I asked Hugo if he would give me a tutorial. Emphatic shake of the head. I asked him for his username. "Mom!" he huffed. "Can't I have one place on social media where you don't follow me?"

Once upon a time, teenagers had diaries with tiny locks to keep their secrets from prying moms. Apparently this is healthy behavior when it comes to developing a sense of self and establishing an identity that is separate from that of the two people responsible for your DNA. But now diaries are extinct. And instead of a diary key, all Mom needs—all anybody needs—is a username. Oh, and permission to see what your own child is up to. (Note to parents: Based on my experience, "But I gave you *life!*" is not reason enough.)

Because the child sitting right next to me (physically, if not virtually) refused to give me a Snapchat lesson, I turned to Owen, who happened to be studying in Spain, for help. Thus ensued a humbling encounter we might call "Middle-Aged Woman Lying in Bed Sees How Old She Looks in Selfies Plus Lots of Photos of Paella." But even after Owen's patient instruction, I still couldn't really figure it out, much less grasp the appeal. Two days later I got a message from Snapchat about...how to use Snapchat. Did my sons send help my way? Was my account flagged because I put in my age when I registered (setting off a Clueless Older Person alert)?

Note to Evan Spiegel and my children: Even getting that app-generated little tutorial did not help me understand. So I suppose you have won. Because my ineptitude did make me a little . . . embarrassed. Which, perhaps, is the point.

Chapter 8
Friends, 100%

"You know what really drives me crazy?" Silvia was saying. "'One hundred percent.' No one says 'Yes' anymore, or 'I agree with you,' or 'I understand.' Everyone just says, *'One hundred percent!'*" She rolled her eyes. "Who started that?"

We were at book group and dinner was in full swing and we had gotten the perfunctory discussion of our most recent reading assignment out of the way as well as all of the necessary, base-touching current events— whose kid had a new job, who just got back from vacation—and the conversation had entered its free-style phase, always the best part. Just nine middle-aged women gathered around a table, wineglasses empty, muffin tops spilling over their waistbands, cry-laughing about some ridiculous aspect of contemporary life. Really, is there anything better?

I met a man the other day who told me he had a comedy routine called "Book Group." He was young, clever, and wearing interesting pants, and he said he performed the show with a friend in Brooklyn. I asked, "Are you making fun of people like me?"

"Oh no!" he quickly replied. "Definitely not." Which I didn't believe. But I also didn't care. Book group may be a cliché to him now, but in twenty-five years he may understand. He may understand why nothing gets in the way of my devotion to book group, my buffer against the modern world and the understanding that I am slowly becoming irrelevant in it.

Until you reach a certain stage of life, friends are 100 percent, and by *100 percent,* I don't mean I'm agreeing with you. I mean you are all in. In childhood, friendship is just about all that matters (sorry, Mom and Dad) and making a new friend is a kind of falling in love: intoxicating, nearly all-consuming. Oh, sure, there's math homework and part-time jobs and parents who require you to take out the garbage and make your bed, but really, most of your time is spent thinking about friends. You seek out friends who fill in the missing parts of yourself. Or at least that's what you did if you were me.

My first best friend was Deidre. Deidre was a marvel. She had a big, ready laugh and a fluffy gray cat named Spike and flawless olive skin. She could do a perfect reverse pike off the diving board at the local pool, where we spent countless summer afternoons, and was a very good dancer, not to mention extremely flexible. Deidre could do so many things I couldn't and was superior to me in ways I could never articulate. She was the life of the party, always doing something that bordered on daredevil-ish, with an impulse to make every day more memorable than the one before. When she got married, she walked down the aisle to "The Girl from Ipanema," for reasons that made sense only to her.

Because Deidre and I met when we were in middle school, it didn't take her long to learn my backstory; there wasn't much to tell. My backstory was a novella, at most, and she could easily absorb it. We remained close friends until we were in our thirties, when the distance between the life she led in Maine and the one I led in New York became more than a few lines of latitude on a map.

I didn't meet Hope until I was twenty-five, and part of what made her spectacular was that she wanted to know my backstory, even though by then it was closer to a Jane Austen novel (not in its wisdom or subtlety but in its length). We met in the bathroom of a New York City fundraiser when she accosted me because she liked my earrings. Hope grew up in Manhattan, in an apartment; her childhood, to me, was a combination of *Corduroy* and *From the Mixed-Up Files of Mrs. Basil E. Frankweiler.* She too was superior in ways I couldn't articulate. She knew about the Hamptons and art galleries and the media. She had thick, curly hair that seemed to have a mind of its own, the kind of hair I'd longed for all my life. Hope introduced me to the most charming little park in New York, the one at Fifth Avenue and 105th Street, which called to mind my favorite book from childhood, *The Secret Garden.* Hope would cut out recipes from *Gourmet* and human-interest stories from *People* magazine and send them to me in the mail with clever annotations; I still have some of them tucked in a file. The best part of Hope was that she saw absurdity everywhere she looked, and she made me see it too. She had a family friend named Harry Buttrick and we had lots of fun with that (*My, you've got a hairy butt, Rick!*). Oh, Hope was just perfect: sophisticated and juvenile at the same time, the most wonderful friend combination there is. And then I moved to Brooklyn and she moved to Princeton, our families and responsibilities grew, and that was the end of that.

• • •

There are friends you lose touch with and friends you break up with, and, if enough years pass, sometimes you don't remember the difference. After Deidre and Hope, I did not fall obsessively in love in the same way with any new friend. I had a husband, and I had children, and that was as much obsession as my tender heart could bear. Now my friendships with Deidre and Hope are like big pieces of costume jewelry that have been passed down to me: Too meaningful to throw out, too outdated to wear. So they sit in a box on a high shelf in my bedroom closet. I rarely look at them, but I always know they're there.

Why does it get harder to make friends as we grow older? Perhaps it's because we can't hear each other the way we could when we were young. When you're young, there is very little competing background noise. As you get older, other voices begin to chime in—partners, kids, bosses, electricians, plumbers, PTA presidents—and soon there is clamor all around you.

If you make a new friend, she must join a very noisy chorus. She will never be the soloist.

And eventually your backstory just gets so long. It becomes the *Encyclopedia Britannica,* for those of you who get that reference. While you would never require a new friend to read the whole thing, the fact that she can't means that she may never fully know you. Which is sad. But that's life. You don't have time to read anyone else's encyclopedia either.

I like to think I am good at friendship. I will listen patiently and will try—and even occasionally succeed—to ask permission before I offer advice. I am never embarrassed or freaked out by crying. I will bring a side dish and laugh at your jokes. I am not cheap when it comes to flowers or wine. I will happily lend you my cupcake tin, my car, my guest room, my child to take in your mail when you are on vacation, provided you pay him a little something. I will do the driving if you don't want to. I will eat wherever you want, really, I don't care, just as long as there's something besides okra. I will make myself available for a walk, as a good friend does.

There are people in this world, however, who are *great* at friendship. And I am not one of them.

Not long ago I read an interview with Clemson football coach Dabo Swinney in which he said, "The way you do anything is the way you do everything." Dabo Swinney seems to be not only super-successful but also a super-nice guy, the kind of person just about anybody would want for a friend. However, I don't agree with his sentiment. The way I feed my dogs, for example, is not the way I feed my friendships. I feed my dogs with vigilance, frequency, and a firm sense of duty. Plus—except during the brief moments when I wonder whether I should be making them homemade meals in my food processor—I believe that I am good at it. In contrast, I feed my friendships with...well...

Unless you are a lunatic/perfect pet owner, feeding a dog takes three minutes, twice a day. Feeding a friendship—oh, I get tired just thinking about it.

And yet friendship makes us human! It's what sustains us! You've seen all of those studies about social networks, how people with strong human ties are happier, yes, but they are also healthier and less likely to be depressed, to have high blood pressure, or to die tomorrow. Friendship, the feeling of generosity and love for your fellow man, the drive to connect with people, is a force that runs through your life like an underground stream. You can't hear the water burble but it's the reason the grass is so green. Until you reach a certain age when perhaps other things demand your attention—such as your two dogs, who probably should be eating homemade food containing kelp powder, which you must order from obscure websites—and friendship seems just so, well, time-consuming that you wander away from that green patch of grass and eventually find yourself in a brown field where it's clear there has not been any water flowing in a very long time.

And then you become sadder and lonelier, unloved and lost, and eventually you won't have anyone to come to your funeral. Even your dogs will be long gone, especially if you never got around to ordering the kelp powder that some website promised would help them live to the age of twenty.

When I was first married I lived in Brooklyn and had one phone, a rotary-dial that sat on a bureau beside an uncomfortable chair in the living room. I had a particular friend, whom I adored then and still adore today, who really, really loved to talk on the phone. And just talk, without a clear purpose, at a rambling pace that made me feel like I had ants crawling all over my body. He called frequently, not to confirm a fact or make plans or thank me for dinner the night before, which was what we all did before texting. He called just to talk. As an expression of friendship. I love this man—he is generous and interesting and has an open-minded way of approaching nearly every aspect of life.

He is a voracious reader with a voice full of laughter, and he remembers parts of my backstory that even I have forgotten. Still, when he called and I answered on the rotary phone, I was stuck there, as if someone had shackled me to the chair with a pair of leg irons. It was excruciating. I began to dread his calls, which I couldn't avoid because caller ID had not been invented yet, and what if it was my parents phoning to say that someone had gotten engaged or fallen off a ladder? And then my husband, ever clever in the gift department, gave me a cordless phone for Christmas. Now when this friend called, I could do something productive while we talked, like water the plants or sort the laundry, and all was right with the world again.

I do not actually believe this is how life should be lived, with productivity as the number-one goal and friendship barely making it into the top five. But it's how I am wired. There has never been a time in my life when I wanted to just sit and talk on the phone. My parents and sisters are exactly the same way, which is why we get along so well. Technology has only made matters worse. I have an old *New Yorker* cartoon tacked up beside my desk that features two guys sitting at a bar and one is saying to the other, "I used to call people, then I got into e-mailing, then texting, and now I just ignore everyone." Exactly.

My sister Claire, who is a therapist, says it is possible to be an extroverted introvert, and maybe that explains why I behave the way I do. Sometimes I get an alert from Facebook that a "friend" is celebrating a birthday, but I ignore it because I'm too lazy to log onto Facebook and the whole thing seems insincere and forced. And then when it's my turn, and I see the number of people who post birthday wishes to me, I'm filled with shame.

Sometimes I skip an opportunity to go out for drinks because I just want to stay home and watch *Pitch Perfect,* wedged in a cozy chair beside a giant dog, even though I've seen that movie half a dozen times and the dog and I will both be asleep before it's over.

Sometimes I meet a new person and even though she is nice and fairly interesting, the thought bubble over my head reads, *I will be okay if I never see you again for the rest of my life.*

Sometimes I see a person I truly love on the train platform and still ignore her, even if I haven't seen her in six months, because I prefer to sit in the quiet car where I can read the paper and not have to socialize. Or it could just be a morning when I hate everyone.

I read an article in the *New York Times* last year that described the importance of "weak ties." Sociologists have come to believe that casual human interactions can be extremely valuable and important to your mental and psychological health. Once upon a time, no one thought it was worth researching the way you interact with your mail carrier, but it turns out that your mail carrier does a lot more for you than deliver the kelp powder that will, for an afternoon, make you feel like a person who has her priorities straight. Your mail carrier is important because she is a low-stakes acquaintance, and low-stakes acquaintances can make us happier and more satisfied. In other words, who needs intense friendships when there's the pharmacist and the dry cleaner and Magdalene at Blue Dog Wines on Wolfs Lane? They know my name, what pills I take, what size I wear, and what kind of wine I prefer. They are helpful and friendly, and interacting with them is always pleasant. That, I sometimes think, can be enough.

But then I think of my toolbox.

There was a time, more than a decade ago, when my husband and I were still defined by optimism, possessing none of the fatalism or jadedness that would come to corrupt our feelings about politics, the NBA draft, or the college application process. It was during these happy, naive days that we took Owen—the eldest, the canary in the coal mine, poor kid, time and again—on a weeklong college tour. He was a high-school junior. On a beautiful spring morning, we pulled into the visitor parking lot on the verdant campus of the southern university that Owen's guidance counselor had recommended we visit because it was a "target school," meaning one that would not reject him and make him want to kill himself.

Before the three of us embarked on the college trip, more experienced parents said, "When your kid steps onto a campus, he just knows." This seemed far-fetched—how do you know anything about a place the second you step out of a car other than whether or not you need an umbrella? But as we turned off the car in the lot on that pretty spring day, a sparkling, bottle-green luxury sedan pulled into the spot beside us. From the sedan emerged two parents and a son, all wearing polo shirts that were wrinkle-free and tucked in. As the eldest child of parents who rarely washed the car and were nothing if not wrinkled and untucked, Owen announced, "I don't like this place. Everybody here looks like a tool."

A *tool.* In our house, if you were a teenage boy, that was the most insulting thing you could say about a person without actually cursing. An etymologist might be able to explain how a word that evokes a solid, enduring, useful object came to represent the thing a high-school junior would least like to be. But I do know that when Owen looked at the tucked-in boy in the university parking lot, his thought process went something like this: *That kid is a tool, this school will be full of tools, I myself am not a tool, therefore I will have zero friends if I end up here.*

What Owen didn't realize is that friends are tools, just not the teenage-boy kind. And we carry a friendship toolbox with us through life. Last winter a neighbor of ours turned sixty and his wife threw a surprise party for him. It was a warm Saturday night and my husband and I didn't have anything else to do, but of course neither of us wanted to go because we never really want to go anywhere. On the way over in the car, I told him, "When I turn sixty, please don't throw a party for me because I don't want anyone to wish they didn't have to come." When we arrived at the party, though, it was filled with old friends we rarely see: Parents whose children, once schoolmates or team-mates of Owen or Hugo, were now either in college or living in city apartments. People whose lives once intersected with ours so often—at elementary-school drop-off, at the Little League parade, at the Halloween pumpkin sale—that for a time we were all traveling together toward a fixed destination. And now we had scattered. Our children had graduated and we had, too, to the next phase of life. There was melancholy, because some friends were missing and because many dreams we held when we were twenty years younger had failed to come true. But I was reminded of the last stanza of Matthew Arnold's poem "Dover Beach," which begins

Ah, love, let us be true
To one another! for the world, which seems
To lie before us like a land of dreams,
So various, so beautiful, so new,
Hath really neither joy, nor love, nor light,
Nor certitude, nor peace, nor help for pain;
And we are here as on a darkling plain

As I stood in the middle of the loud, happy swirl of people I thought: *Let us be true to one another.* And when we left, I turned to my husband and said, "I'm really glad we came."

Back to tools. They are, or so I've heard, what distinguishes you and me from the badger and the blue jay and the Alaskan king crab—we humans know how to use tools to take a situation that is suboptimal and make it better. Owen wasn't old enough to know this as he stood in that parking lot at age seventeen, and he's probably not old enough to know it at twenty-five, but the fact of the matter is that friends, old or new, are tools of tremendous utility, variety, and importance. That crowded sixtieth birthday party contained a friendship toolbox that had served me for decades. You have one too. Your friends keep you level and help you remain anchored when you feel like you are slipping. They prop you up and take your measure and set you straight. They illuminate the path before you.

Which is why my book group is so vital to my well-being. We have been meeting once a month or so for the past twenty years. We are all roughly the same age, and each of us has two or three children except for Mary, who has nine! We take turns hosting, and the hostess makes dinner. The dinner is extremely important. Few people I know have dinner parties anymore, which is quite unfortunate, since at a dinner party you don't spend the whole night standing up. But my book-group meetings are dinner parties, with hors d'oeuvres and cloth napkins and often more than one dessert because, thank God, no one is ever on a soul-killing, kooky diet. Mary, who is otherwise indefatigable, always orders Chinese food because nine children + full-time job = takeout. Missy has incredible style and makes these grapes rolled in goat cheese and chopped pistachios that are so surprising and good, you could cry. Raylene has so many funny stories that she should have a TV show or be a stand-up comic or both. No matter what you do or where you go, it always turns out that Ann Marie has done it or visited it first. Sharene is loyal and curious and so discreet, plus she has fabulous art on her walls. Tina is the strongest, most organized woman imaginable, and Jenny—gorgeous and wise—has a voice like a warm bath. And Silvia is simply the coolest of all of us. Aside from when I am with my two sisters, I never laugh so hard as I do on the nights of book group. Within a matter of minutes the conversation can range from Ruth Bader Ginsburg to Richard Chamberlain to why in the world anyone would ever want to get a neck tattoo. We came together when our children were in diapers, and when I went to our most recent meeting, I looked at the faces around the table, illuminated by candlelight, and thought of all the things we had weathered together: divorce, illness, death. Sick children, sick parents, sick spouses. Downsizing houses and losing jobs. We have become a bit—just a bit!—jowly. We are thicker in the middle, and we all have hi-Helens. We greet each other with enthusiasm and tenderness and when we say goodbye, it is with a full body hug, a hug-like-you-mean-it hug, because we're old enough to realize that you just never know.

These women became my friends in adulthood and

Chapter 9
Things Fall Apart

When we go to bed at night and want to keep our dog Jill in the kitchen, we have to block the doorway with a chair. If we don't, Jill wanders the house at all hours, sleeping wherever her determined little heart desires, flattening cushions and depositing stiff black fur on the upholstery and occasionally even relieving herself on the sisal, impossible-to-clean, might-as-well-throw-it-out-now dining-room rug. Our Jill is an angel and a devil and simultaneously the best and worst dog we have ever had.

But Jill's story is one for another time. Because we're

here to talk about my toenail. The other morning I was moving the dog-blocking chair from the kitchen doorway back to its rightful place in the living room when I lost my balance and knocked the big toe of my left foot against the heel of my right. Naturally, my toenail broke in half.

This is how bad the situation has become. There are parts of my body that seem sapped of all strength, beginning with my toenails. It's not like I hit my toenail very hard—I just tapped it against a *flesh-covered part of my own body*. Friendly fire, as it were. And I don't believe my big toenail would have broken twenty years ago. But over time, certain things lose their zest for life. In the inventory of body parts, the left big toenail is fairly insignificant. And, unlike my heart or brain, it can be fixed in my own home after a quick visit to the kitchen computer. My sons make fun of me because my answer to most questions is "Just Google it," but I ask you: Where else but Google can I learn at 6:45 on a Sunday morning that I can DIY a toenail repair with a tea bag and some Gorilla Glue?

As I said, though, the toenail is a small concern. Compared to, say, my ABDOMEN, which—as discussed in chapter 1—is a region of my body prone to betrayal. Like many high-school students across America, I was once forced to read "The Second Coming," by

William Butler Yeats, and I had no idea what it meant, nor did I care. I read it now—*Things fall apart; the center cannot hold*—and two concerns spring to mind: (1) U.S. politics, and (2) my ABDOMEN.

Are you ever foul-tempered for reasons you can't fathom? Sometimes I find myself at nine thirty on an otherwise normal morning feeling very cross, and I go through a little checklist in my head, searching for the cause.

- Sleepless night? No
- Mad at husband? No
- Worried about kids? No
- Problem at work? No
- Thinking about politics? No

And then, after rooting around in the dark chambers of my brain, I hit on it: it's my ABDOMEN.

I don't write ABDOMEN in capital letters as a literary device or a sign of emphasis or because I'm shouting. ABDOMEN is in capital letters because that is how important my ABDOMEN is to my well-being. Some women talk about bad hair days. Bad hair days aren't really a problem for me, because I hate my hair every day. I've given up on hair. It is beyond my power to make it thicker, longer, stronger, better.

My ABDOMEN, however, I can control, even as it controls me. This is not a situation I have to take lying down. Although lying down—that is, lying down without also doing a plank or fifty sit-ups—is part of the problem. I've seen pictures of Courteney Cox and Demi Moore in their bikinis. I've seen women who aren't famous, just women my age whom I know, in bikinis on Instagram and IRL, as the kids say, who have flat stomachs because they work at it. Both of my sisters have flat stomachs, which just feels unfair. Particularly because once upon a time, I had a flat stomach too. This is within my power! But there's wine and TV and rhubarb pie and Jill, who loves to plant herself next to me, press her body against mine, and silently will me to sit on the floor and scratch her ears when instead I could be strengthening my core. These things all get in the way of me taking control of the ABDOMEN.

I used to work with a woman who had no children and who was thin and fit except for a little poofy stomach. She might recognize herself when she reads this and feel hurt when I admit that looking at her poofy stomach gave me a little thrill of schadenfreude. She was my age, and her stomach suggested that maybe midsection expansion was inevitable and (sadly) one thing I couldn't blame on the kids.

I used to work with another woman who was

very skinny, super-chic, bawdy, and hilarious. She is the person who taught me what FUPA means (fat upper-pussy area, in case you didn't know either). This woman and I worked together for literally decades but FUPA is the detail that lingers. I remember her fondly in part because, as skinny as she was, FUPA was apparently a matter of concern for her too.

I pass women of all shapes and sizes on the street, women who have poofy stomachs or FUPA or big round bellies like Major League Baseball umpires. I wonder whether their midsections bother them as much as mine does me. Is Sophia Loren bothered by her stomach? Maybe if I move to Italy and wear plunging wrap dresses and take my meals outdoors in an olive grove, I will be at peace with my ABDOMEN. Until I can move to Italy, though, I fear my foul mood will continue.

My ABDOMEN isn't the only thing that cannot hold. There's the body, and then there's the world it inhabits. Here are a few things that have recently fallen apart in my life: the car, the bathroom pipes, the circulator that supplies heat to the kitchen, and my son Axel's cello. This list in and of itself is not particularly impressive. But when you add the body falling apart, you reach a tipping point that makes life—which I am meant to value more every day, I know!—feel, well, like too much to bear. In the space of the past two weeks, I also found out that I have a little spot of basal cell skin cancer on my forehead and, per my dentist, need crowns on two teeth, the two with fractures so pronounced that even I can see them when Dr. Crowe shoves that little round mirror into my mouth. Beneath the fractured teeth, you never really know what's going on. Although I have a suspicion: If history is any guide, it's a quiet, dangerous, bacterial rumble, like the beginnings of a volcanic eruption, except instead of lava, what eventually flies out is hundred-dollar bills. Because the second Dr. Crowe seals everything with crowns, I'm going to need a root canal. Eight dental visits and five thousand dollars later, I will be as good as new. You know how some streets of Greenwich Village were once cow paths? Well, I'm making my mark on my adopted city by wearing a path from the dentist on West Fifty-Ninth Street to the endodontist on West Forty-Fourth. I'm pretty sure that, by the time all my teeth are crowned or I'm dead, whichever comes first, the city's department of transportation will have paved a new road in my honor.

Or not.

Everywhere I go these days, someone is scolding me about deferred maintenance. There's the dentist, of course. The plumber scolds me for not keeping the water in the bathroom faucet running when the day-time temperature dips below eighteen degrees—don't I remember the last time the pipes froze? And Jeff the mechanic scolds me each time I see him. Whenever our car goes into the shop, which has got to be more frequently than the national average, my husband and I have a polite little argument about who has to pick it up once it's fixed. It's always at the end of a workday and picking up the car means fifteen minutes of listening to Jeff express his disappointment in you before you are allowed to pay the bill and leave. When it comes to cars, my husband and I employ the same approach we use on pets, good babysitters, and close friends: hold on to them for as long as possible while undoubtedly ignoring them more than we should. We don't wash our cars often enough, and at any given time you will find the cupholders filled with empty coffee mugs, broken reading glasses, or, this week, crushed tortilla chips, courtesy of our son Owen, who seems to eat all of his meals on I-95. The car that most recently needed repairing was a fifteen-year-old SUV that had been as loud as a Jet Ski for the past few years, which didn't seem to concern anyone except passengers who got in it for the first time and wondered why they couldn't hold a conversation in a normal tone. But now the car had developed a new sound, a mysterious garage and attach to a car you aren't going to be driving for a while in order to prevent the battery from dying. It costs a hundred dollars and I'm hoping someone will invent the human equivalent for me.

For the record, my husband and I are also sensible people adhering to the golden mean as best we can. We vote and pay our mortgage on time and have produced three boys who never ingested anything poisonous as toddlers or spent the night in jail as adults. True, there have been trips to the emergency room, totaled cars, and written contracts involving marijuana use, but we're not going to get into that now. The world is full of ding-a-lings and I like to think we're not part of that crowd.

But maintenance has never been as important as reading the newspaper, scrolling through message boards devoted to college basketball, or hunting down the recipe for the cake I once had at a restaurant in Birmingham, Alabama, the best cake I've ever eaten in my life. As we trundle through middle age, most of us can handle the diminishment of vitality and the fuzziness of memory and the fact that we've lost so much collagen that the wrinkles from the pillow stay imprinted on our faces for far too long after we've gotten out of bed. It's the amount of time we need to spend on maintenance that is the most irritating. How do people over sixty-five have time for anything but doctor's visits?

Which brings me back to my teeth. In addition to the fractures, I have a persistent pain above one of my top molars. Have I called Dr. Crowe or scheduled an appointment with the endodontist? Of course not. I'm not ready to trigger that particular time-consuming chain reaction. Because the last time my mouth felt like this, it led to a root canal on a rainy Saturday when I was supposed to be getting ready to host a dinner party. Once he had finished, the excellent and quite thorough endodontist announced that he had done an "A minus or B plus" job and he wasn't satisfied with that. Two or three or maybe twelve appointments later, he was satisfied and I felt like I had lost a year of my life. Not to mention enough money for a trip to Aruba.

Advil—that is to say, denial—is just so much faster.

To borrow the wisdom of T. S. Eliot, the secret is to care and not to care, while not scaring the younger people around you. Six years ago, in a moment of startling conscientiousness, I got a colonoscopy exactly when I was supposed to, at age fifty. "The colonoscopy isn't bad—*it's the prep!*" If I had a dollar for every time a friend said that to me, I could pay for twenty root canals. I so dreaded the Prep that when I finally had to drink that awful stuff—and manage the consequences—

it didn't actually seem so bad. The procedure itself wasn't terrible either. And because I had it done in Greenwich, Connecticut, where my dirty Jet Ski car sat in the parking lot cheek by jowl with Mercedes and Jaguars and other cars whose cupholders were not filled with tortilla chips, my gentle post-colonoscopy care included two perfectly toasted pieces of thick raisin bread, slathered with butter. Then my husband threw me in the Jet Ski and drove me home and that was that.

What no one warned me about, however, was that it would take a while for...things...to go back to normal. The day after my colonoscopy, it was my turn for monthly lunch duty at Axel's elementary school. Lunch duty, for a parent, means sticking on a name tag and patrolling the long, crowded tables, helping kids open their milk cartons, course-correcting those who can't keep their hands to themselves, and resisting the urge to rescue what seems like hundreds of unopened bags of baby carrots from the trash. I always loved lunch duty, because seeing what was inside kids' lunch boxes was like taking a field trip into the kitchens and value systems of half my town. If you know the children's book *Bread and Jam for Frances,* one of my all-time favorites, you will understand what I mean: There are lunch boxes with grape jelly on squishy white bread and lunch boxes with four-course meals.

with a heavy sigh and defeat in his voice, "Well, she's getting married today."

I hadn't seen Mrs. Rossi in a while, and at lunch duty on the day after my colonoscopy, I was listening to her tell me how she had celebrated her recent birthday when suddenly I felt like I had been stabbed in the stomach.

"I can't believe I'm twenty-nine," she was saying. "It feels so old."

"Mmmm-hmmm," I said, pinching my side and bending over just slightly, hoping she wouldn't notice.

"I'm almost thirty!"

The pain got sharper; I pinched harder.

"And so many of my friends are getting pregnant!"

I nodded, bending over a bit more. "It's a very exciting time of your life," I said through clenched teeth. Until that point, I hadn't given much thought to what the previous day's procedure actually involved. Now I imagined my colon, hidden and slippery and as long as a python, filled with angry little pockets of air that were fighting each other to get out.

"I know," she said with a smile. "I just hope...um, are you okay?"

By this point I was hinged ninety degrees at the waist and looking at her shoes. "I'm fine," I croaked. "I had a colonoscopy yesterday."

She gave me a confused look.

"I think it might just take a couple of days to recover," I said. Under no circumstances would I utter the word *gas* in the elementary-school lunchroom. My friend Beth says one of the worst things about getting older is "the surprise fart." The python in my body was planning something much worse.

Mrs. Rossi regarded me sympathetically, the way you would an elderly dog whose back legs no longer work and so its owner has MacGyvered a wheelie device to its hindquarters so it can pretend to walk with dignity down the street. You root for the creature while feeling pity that it has to be seen like that in public. She nodded as if she understood—even though she was only twenty-nine, even though she probably wouldn't have to think about colonoscopies for decades—which was what made her such an excellent teacher, not to mention the woman Axel wanted to marry. "Maybe you should go home," she said.

"Yes," I replied.

Despite appearances, both literal and figurative, I would not want to be twenty-nine again. There is so much uncertainty in that time of life, so much self-doubt, so many hours spent wondering where your life is going and whether you are proceeding at the right speed as friends whoosh by you in the passing lane. And there is so much you don't know. Some of what you learn between the ages of twenty-nine and fifty-six is wonderful and some of it makes the world feel scrambled and cruel. But knowledge, as they say, is power. Even if there are days you'd like to give that power back.

There is one thing I envy about my twenty-nine-year-old self, however: the bedtime routine. I think wistfully of when, at the end of the day, I could just wash my face, brush my teeth, and collapse into bed. Now shutting down operations for the night is a complicated endeavor, what with the lotions and creams and ointments and pills and the glass of water next to the bottle of thyroid medication on the bedside table and finding just the right pillow for the stiff neck, not to mention the time devoted to examining my gums, which, after a lifetime of too-vigorous brushing, may have receded so much that Dr. Crowe is going to have to repair them with little pieces of cadaver, which is what happened to my father and my friend Kim. I'm sure it is a brilliant solution, but that really feels like you've crossed a line, when you've got part of another person's dead body in your mouth.

And where is my top lip going? It's a mystery. I worry that in fifteen years it will disappear altogether, having slowly eroded from overuse, like Machu Picchu.

Come to think of it, the whole mouth area becomes something of a sad World Heritage Site once you reach your fifties. In addition to the disappearing top lip, there are the little vertical lines that ring your mouth like barbed wire, even if you apply Blistex religiously and have never smoked a day in your life.

And then there are the elevens.

Last February my family hosted a potluck dinner for all the people on our block. It was a fun party; our neighbors are reasonable, warm people with interesting jobs and children who make eye contact, and some of them are excellent cooks. One family even brought cookies decorated with house numbers on them— a pink-frosted, heart-shaped treat for each household. These cookie decorators were the newest people on the block, and while some might regard the gesture as show-offy or desperate, I found it overachieving in all the best ways. They (overachievers!) also made a coconut cake from an Ina Garten recipe that was the second-most delicious cake I've had in all my life, after the one from Birmingham, which I still haven't reproduced.

Anyway I was rushing around, doing hostess stuff, hurrying back and forth from the kitchen to the dining room with platters of *The Silver Palate*'s Chicken Marbella (remember that? It's as good today as it was thirty years ago) and gravy boats of sauce and trivets for hot casserole dishes when my neighbor Elasah gently grasped my arm, looked at me with concern, and said, "Is everything all right?"

"Pardon?"

"Is there anything I can do?" she asked. And then I understood. It's my face—specifically, my permafrown. Something happened between my thirties and forties: I developed an *eleven,* or two parallel lines above the bridge of my nose (not to be confused with *elevenses,* which is the second breakfast people in the UK eat and just further proof that we should all be living in Buckingham Palace). When you have an eleven, your resting face is a frown, and you look angry or confused or in need of help from your neighbor even if the potluck is going well and you feel just fine. Everyone in my family has an eleven. You should see my father; he's now eighty-one and when he's not smiling, he looks like he wants to run you over with his car.

So, to review: receding gums, disappearing upper lip, smoker's lines, the eleven. Years of editing women's magazines have provided me with countless ways to combat these problems. Some are cheap and ineffective (sleep with a silk pillowcase!), others expensive and effective (Juvéderm!), still others super-weird (snail slime! urine therapy! sheep placenta!). And that's just for the territory above the neck.

Which brings me back to the ABDOMEN, where there is breaking news. Remember my two sisters with their flat stomachs? Claire, who is fifty-one, lives on a little farm that requires her to do a lot of core-strengthening manual labor, and Valerie, fifty-three, is just lucky that way. Or she was. The other afternoon Valerie and I were talking on the phone about weekend plans and birthdays and homesick college students when suddenly she said, "I need to start working out more because I can't get rid of this STOMACH." Her voice rose as she continued. "It's driving me crazy. Is it just middle age?"

"Well—"

"I did paleo for two weeks and I lost a pound and a half but the STOMACH is still there." Now she was practically shouting.

"Welcome to my—"

"Is this just my body now? Is this just it, like, forever? What am I supposed to do," she yelled, "just *live with it?*"

I smiled in sympathy because I love my sister and because I was grateful that she wouldn't hear the schadenfreude in my voice. "Yes," I replied.

Chapter 10

My Own Style of She Shed: More Vodka, Less Gingerbread Trim

It is a truth universally acknowledged that a woman in possession of three boys, two dogs, and a husband who never turns off the TV must be in want of a she shed.

We can simultaneously applaud and blame Pinterest for bringing these little structures into perfect, peppy, inferiority-producing focus. Maybe a teeny backyard building really can provide an escape from the countless demands in the average woman's life and help her find her true self again. That's appealing, right?

But the more pictures I see of she sheds, the more they scare me. If this is a woman's answer to a man cave, I'd rather be a man. Absent are the foosball tables, the beer on tap, the elaborate sound systems and exercise equipment. Instead women get shingle siding, lavender paint, window boxes, lace curtains, and an abundance of gingerbread trim. These decorative sign-posts are each fine in isolation. But cram them together and throw a glue-gun-fueled craft project on top and the result is a gigantic estrogen explosion. Just imagine a Nancy Meyers movie with Beatrix Potter doing the set design. We might as well force those who have a Y chromosome to move to another planet.

Which I'll admit can be an appealing thought if, like me, you are the mother of three boys. I have a dear friend whose therapist once told him that he starts metaphorical fires just so he can put them out. I have a similar problem in that I keep having boys and then just want to get away from them. Why? Because they need me too much.

When I was a new mother, I believed that my boys would seek me out for my unique life wisdom and deep insight into the really important things (if a bird in the hand truly is worth two in the bush; whether virtue actually is its own reward; why women never get tired of the six-hour *Pride and Prejudice* starring Colin Firth).

But no. My boys need me, and me alone, to find the crapola they have scattered all over the house.

I think *What to Expect When You're Expecting* should stop devoting so much attention to labor and delivery (after all, they are fairly brief episodes in the grand scheme of things) and issue an updated edition with a chapter titled "Things Your Children Will Never Be Able to Locate Without Your Help (and Yes, Those Things Are Probably Upstairs)." I, for one, would have been much more prepared for the joys of motherhood if I had read such a chapter when I was pregnant. Instead, I greet each day with the vague panic of not knowing when I am going to have to produce a missing shin guard with only three minutes' notice because the soccer game actually starts half an hour earlier than Dad thought. It's like waking up every day in a movie filled with hidden predators. If the people in the audience know when they're going to pop out and scare the hell out of me, they're not saying.

Which brings me to my latest invention: Mom's Little Panic Room.™ Perfect for the woman who doesn't have time for window boxes and hates gingerbread trim but still needs an impenetrable escape from the terrifying demands placed on her by disorganized children. I'm pretty sure this is a product that's going to catch on. Imagine a Kevlar-reinforced bunker with its own communication system and a special hatch in the roof for the delivery of everyday essentials, such as sleeping masks and vodka gimlets. Instead of craft supplies, Mom's Little Panic Room™ will have custom cubbies well stocked with all the things that are constantly going missing in the average American household because no one (read: children, husbands) puts them back where they belong—nail clippers, flashlights, Scotch tape, AA batteries, and pens with caps.

Clever mothers everywhere understand that laziness nearly always trumps need when it comes to missing shin guards, which means if a child is forced to walk all the way outside and penetrate Mom's Little Panic Room™ in order to get help, well, chances are he can find that shin guard on his own. No more learned helplessness—and plenty of time for Mom to watch all six hours of *Pride and Prejudice*. Straight through!

Now all I need is someone to fund my idea. I'm imagining a disorganized young tech entrepreneur who needs a surrogate mother. Oh, and someone to find the keys to his Tesla.

no wild turkeys, no nesting eagle pair, only the wind in the tall pines and enough puddles to keep the Labs happy. Because it was spring and because it was the Adirondacks, there was little color in the brush on either side of our gravel lane other than the occasional fuzzy red sumac. No noise either, except when the branches caught the wind and made a sound that my suburban ears always interprets as a car coming until I realize it's exactly the opposite. Each time I walk the dogs down the road, I notice something new about them that gives me a little tug of joy. This time it was that when Jill—our new puppy, this sweet crazy girl who was mending our hearts—well, when Jill ran hard and fast enough, her tail made an imperfect circle in the air, like an inexperienced cowboy with a furry black lasso.

We stopped at the empty lot on our way home. The grass was still brown but clear of snow, the gentle slope down to the water uninterrupted but for the two boats on trailers, shrink-wrapped in white and waiting for summer. After the dogs chased each other around the lot—the puppy performing an acrobatic side roll whenever the older dog got her pinned, dancing away from him and then circling back for more—they headed for the water. Although the lake was frozen, there was a three-foot-wide section of open water along the shore. As I walked toward the edge, the dogs ventured out onto the ice. Within seconds, Iggy fell through. Jill, following him, soon fell through too. They were about ten feet from shore. Iggy did not like to swim—did not, in fact, seem to know that he could swim, although I assume some sort of canine instinct kicked in as he pawed the ice, trying to get purchase. They had walked on the ice just two days before; did he remember that? Did he wonder, *Wait, this isn't how it's supposed to go?* But it was April, and it had been raining, and neither Iggy nor his owners had received the *How Not to Be an Idiot* manual from the friendly local real estate agent when she sold us the lot at the other end of the gravel road six years earlier. I suppose the manual has some sort of chart to instruct responsible dog owners on how to figure out when the ice is too melted for canine and human foot traffic. Maybe someday I will get my hands on the manual and then will never again do dumb things like tangle the water-ski rope in the boat's propeller, or try to hike the Spectacle Pond trail in March without spikes on the bottom of my boots, or let my dogs walk out on the melting ice.

I called Iggy to the shore, first in a friendly, encouraging tone, then in a strangled, angry cry. By now Jill had positioned herself on Iggy's back, more or less, and they both stopped struggling and just looked at me. How cold was the water? How long would it take for the cold to immobilize a dog? Would I watch his head go under without doing anything? Not again.

I was wearing my orange ski jacket and I hastily threw it onto the shore. I took off my watch—the splurge watch that I had bought myself for my fiftieth birthday—and threw it on top of my coat. The water was very clear at the shore and I stepped carefully onto celadon rocks at the lake's edge, then deeper up to my waist, until I was a few feet from the dogs. Was it incapacitatingly cold? I didn't know. All I knew was that the dogs were just staring at me, immobile. They looked oddly calm, and I remembered the title of an old Stevie Smith poem, "Not Waving but Drowning." Were they just hanging out, or were they quietly panicking in their laconic Labrador retriever way, not-waving-but-drowning? Still calling to Iggy, I chopped through the ice with my forearms, making a channel connecting the dogs to the shore. I grabbed Iggy's collar and pulled him to the channel. Predictably, Jill charged past him and clambered up onto land. Iggy moved more slowly, getting to shore and then seeming not to know how to get back on it. For a few moments he stood in the water, collecting himself. Finally he made it onto the brown grass, as did I, soaking from the waist down, jeans shiny with water, water squishing in my hiking shoes, strangely warm as I walked the quarter of a mile back to the house. The dogs resumed their play, chasing each other around the empty lot as they made their way up the hill, maybe happy to be alive, most likely just energized by the cold. I texted my husband and two older sons to tell them what had happened. *Too much trauma with that lake* was Hugo's immediate reply.

Oh my God, you'd think I would have known better! I didn't wonder until later whether there was someone across the lake wearing a plaid flannel shirt and Carhartt work pants—worn not as a forest-glam style statement but for actual work—watching the whole scene through his binoculars. *Goddamn flatlander,* he would have thought to himself. *When will she ever learn?*

• • •

Sometimes when we have nothing else to argue about, my husband, three sons, and I debate which of our dogs has been the smartest. Over the past fifteen years we have owned four, all Labrador retrievers released as puppies from Guiding Eyes for the Blind, made available for adoption as pets when, at eight weeks old, they failed to demonstrate the exact mix of measurable traits needed to succeed as service dogs. And when the members of my family debate which of our four dogs was the smartest—well, Rebel's name just never comes up.

A longtime Lab owner once told me that there is an expression: You train a black Lab with a newspaper, a yellow Lab with a stick, and a chocolate Lab with a brick. Whoever made that observation never met Rebel, a dim-witted black pup with shining, depthless eyes—alien eyes, my sons called them, because they came of age in an iPhone world, and Rebel's eyes did bear a funny resemblance to those of the alien emoji. We brought Rebel home four days before Christmas in 2015 and found that what he lacked in brains, he made up for in heart, or at least in affection, since he believed that there was nothing you could ever want more than to have him plop down on your lap, your knees, your feet. His general willingness, his malleability, was something we both marveled at and pitied. You could sit in a chair and pull him onto your lap, with his back against your thighs, and he'd lie there belly up, perfectly still. You could take hold of his front legs and pull him around and around the kitchen island, his back legs splayed like he was a spatchcocked chicken, and he'd let you. You could put medicinal eyedrops in his eyes or rub antibiotic ointment on his chin or give him a brisk shampoo in the cold water of the backyard hose and he would just stand there, making occasional eye contact, waiting for it to be over.

The best photograph we have of Rebel was taken on

his second Christmas with us, when he was just over a year old. He was sleeping by the fire, and I draped a sheet of shiny gold wrapping paper over his side, tied a loose green bow around his front leg, put a silver bow on his collar and a red bow on his tail and a big white bow on his right ear. He didn't move a muscle. Why would he? He trusted me. He loved me.

Oh, did Rebel love his people. When he heard you coming in the front door, he would grab a toy and trot over to greet you with it, like the cliché housewife with a martini. His favorite was made of felt, a green stem with a sunflower on the end. When I bought it, it squeaked, but Rebel was an expert at removing squeaking mechanisms within the first ten minutes of owning a new toy. When he came to the door he would hold the sunflower stem sideways in his mouth, like Pepé Le Pew. It was his own silent, irresistible come-on. Occasionally he would pick up his bone-shaped chew toy and grip it in his teeth like a cigar. He would stare at us, holding the pose, and we would take pictures and laugh.

Rebel chewed just about anything crunchy he could get into his mouth. He would chew ice and sticks and mulch and pine cones and plastic Poland Spring bottles. He chewed baseboard molding and the mullions on a French door. He chewed a hole in his faux-leather dog bed so he could get to the green pillow stuffing inside it, which proved too fluffy to be satisfying. He chewed rags and dog leashes and the small Ikea shearling rug that I mistakenly thought would provide a nice, comfy liner for his crate.

He did not chew Iggy. Instead, he would chase his canine big brother around the dining-room table and around the backyard picnic table and around the Japanese maple in our yard until all of my beautiful lilies of the valley planted beneath it were worn down into a slick circle of shredded green foliage. That bothered me. But only a little, because watching the two of them run, whether side by side or in chase, gave me a feeling of joy that was so simple and so pure that I forgot everything else for a while, including the integrity of my garden.

Rebel was smaller, sweeter, more mellow than any dog we'd ever had. And he was different from our previous dogs in that he was actually brave enough—or dumb enough—to swim. Which seemed like a terrific stroke of luck, at least for a while.

Oh, Rebel. If character is fate, then he stayed in character until the end. He never became a service dog, but he ultimately did provide a service. In his dopiness, in his trust, and in his mysterious demise, he confirmed that the Labrador retriever's worldview—strangers are simply friends you haven't met yet—can spread to other species too. And also that in every tragedy, large or small, there are moments of remarkable grace.

• • •

In the southeast corner of New York State's Adirondack Park there is a small, brown board-and-batten house with green-framed windows and a black metal roof. It sits on a steep lot above a little lake, and I own it with my younger sister Valerie. Placed side by side, Valerie and I are like a Venn diagram with a 30 percent section of overlap. We have the same voice and the same hair color, made blonder every couple of months by the same colorist. We are both in long marriages to tall men; we both have resting faces that tend slightly toward a frown. We have both given birth only to sons, meaning we have no one to prom-dress-shop for, no one to teach about tampons and Title IX, no one to notice or point out, half meanly, half helpfully, when we start growing random old-lady hairs from our chins. It's just me and Val and a whole lot of testosterone.

Valerie is the COO of a big fashion retailer and her heart beats only thirty times per minute and she loves to watch football on TV, but those are just three of the ways she's different from me. She's also much more organized and much cleaner. She owns a label maker and actually uses it. She washes the covers on her dog beds with enthusiasm and regularity; I wash mine only if they are covered in mud or if Iggy rolls in something dead, one of his special talents, and then rubs that smell all over the dog bed to the point that you can't be in the same room with it.

Somewhere in middle adulthood, one of us cooked up the potentially relationship-demolishing idea of buying a lake house together. We are what Adirondack residents refer to as *flatlanders*—people who live in the suburbs of New York City for the good schools and easy Metro North commute into Grand Central Station but long to live someplace where there isn't a Panera Bread around every corner. One weekend in 2011 our two families were skiing at Gore Mountain in the southern Adirondacks and I struck up a conversation in the lodge with a skier named Peter who told me all about the little lake where he had a house. Peter encouraged me to take his phone number, which I did, but I never got his last name because all of a sudden Axel, who was four years old and wearing a one-piece ski outfit, executed a spectacular klutzy move: he stumbled in his heavy ski boots, knocked into the table, and spilled hot chocolate all over himself. I'm not even sure how he did it, but somehow the hot chocolate (which, luckily, had cooled) poured down from the tippy-top of his head all over his little body, like brown volcanic lava. I did the only logical thing, which was to laugh my head off. Axel was too young to realize that we were laughing at him—truly, just about the best phase of parenting.

The following summer, Valerie rented a house for a week on Peter's lake and there happened to be a six-acre lot on the market. She and I drove over to look at it from one side, then kayaked to examine it from the other. We walked up and down the slope, dodging thorny blackberry bushes and rock formations that may or may not have been bobcat dens, too clueless to consider whether there was an iPhone app that measured steepness. In our flatlander lives, steepness was not something we considered very often unless we were counting subway stairs. Which is why we went ahead and bought the lot and built a house that is separated from the lake by half an acre of steps.

Building the house required nine thousand decisions, and Valerie made eighty-nine hundred of them. Which was fine with me. I contributed when I needed to, mostly serving as flatlander communications director. Like when we got the e-mail from the neighbor about the giant pieces of rock our builder had inadvertently blasted onto the frozen lake, creating a huge danger for snowmobilers. That was illuminating—who knew rock could fly that far? Or the time the town administrator called about inspecting our dock because a snoopy neighbor had (inaccurately) reported to him that we used pressure-treated wood, which was against the rules we were trying so hard to learn.

My best contribution to the shared enterprise came from the flagship Anthropologie store a block from my Manhattan office where I found these little hand-painted juice glasses featuring two blond girls in a canoe on a lake surrounded by pine trees; above the girls are painted the words HELLO FRIEND. The glasses were like a little miracle, a sign, cementing in my mind the wisdom and inevitability of my sister and me building a lake house together. Since then, for both of our families, the Adirondacks have been a refuge and a magic show, relaxing and stimulating all at once. We have no rules about who uses the house when, meaning on some weekends or holidays you will find two or three people there and at other times it looks like the entire cast of *The Sound of Music* has moved in.

On that Christmas of 2016, when we had had Rebel for a year, there were eleven humans and four big shedding dogs crammed into the little house by the lake. My family of five, Valerie's family of four, our two parents, and the dog quartet: Iggy and Rebel and Val's two golden retrievers. December 31 was a gray Saturday, and the members of our group were scattered; some were skiing, some were running errands, some were on the lake, where the younger kids had cleared off the snow to create a small hockey rink. They were smacking the puck around when my husband headed out with Iggy and Rebel for a walk. The lake—a 440-acre imperfect oval—was dotted with cross-country skiers, ice fishermen huddled on stools, and larger packs of skaters, some who'd cleared impressively big rinks. And dogs. Dogs everywhere, because in the Adirondacks, of course, everyone has a dog.

I went with our son Owen to Price Chopper in Warrensburg to buy cheese for fondue and wine for New Year's Eve and black-eyed peas for hoppin' John, which I planned to make later that day—an annual tradition to ensure that we would have good luck in the coming year. As I stood in the canned-food aisle searching for the black-eyed peas, my husband called. "Will you come home as soon as you can?" he asked, an edge in his voice. "I can't find Rebel."

And somewhere in the cosmos, someone whispered, *Poof.* Just like that, a dog was gone.

The eleven of us spent the rest of that Saturday, as the weather grew colder and darkness fell, walking and driving on the icy local roads, calling the puppy's name. We looked on as people began to celebrate

New Year's Eve inside their snug houses, light from the windows spilling out in elongated rectangles onto the snow. Rebel had become like air: nowhere and everywhere, invisible but all around us. Every possibility— that he was lost, that he was lying injured beside the road, that he was in someone's house, that he was under the ice—was unbearable.

• • •

Beneath a window in my kitchen I have a little ceramic dish that I walk by more than a dozen times a day. On the dish is printed this command: BE THE PERSON YOUR DOG THINKS YOU ARE. This is a noble goal that is also completely impossible. My dogs think I am happy and generous and full of love for all God's creatures when in fact I am judgmental and impatient and the list of the members of my species who annoy me is long and varied:

- the lazy
- the indecisive
- people who chew with their mouths open
- bigots
- braggarts
- chauvinists

- narcissists
- pessimists
- the pathologically incurious
- the stingy
- litterbugs
- close-talkers
- scowling salespeople
- people who don't say thanks when you hold the door open for them
- people who don't give you a little grateful wave when you let them go first at a four-way stop
- conversation-monopolizers
- ingrates
- mumblers
- people who can't be bothered to respond to your e-mail
- the humorless
- the pompous
- people who walk slowly in the center of the sidewalk so you can't pass on either side
- parents who talk about their children as if they were the only children ever born to anyone in the history of mankind
- obsessive selfie-takers
- the unreliable
- liars

Before we lost Rebel, the list was twice as long. But shortly after he disappeared I read a little book called *On Kindness*. In it, authors Adam Phillips and Barbara Taylor write, "Kindness is a way of knowing people beyond our understanding of them." Which helps explain, perhaps, how a dog's disappearance forced his owner to rethink her whole worldview.

Although we had spent only three years on the lake, word of our loss spread quickly. Neighbors (most of whom I didn't know) began to e-mail me with stories: About that time their black Lab pushed open the screen door of an unoccupied camp and couldn't get out again. That time another black Lab ran away to hang out with the thoroughbreds at Chestertown Farm. That time a yellow Lab got trapped in an empty bedroom suite and survived for five days drinking water out of the toilet. Each of these stories provided both a happy ending and a new way of searching for Rebel that, though fruitless, felt somehow like a near miss. With each near miss, our hearts would rise and then sink again, lower each time, like a birthday-party balloon slowly losing its helium. Each dead end took us closer to something, but none of us were sure what.

I repeated the particulars of Rebel's disappearance countless times: My husband was walking south on the lake, the expanse of frozen water on his left and land on his right. The shoreline was mostly frozen except around a few of the docks. My husband saw nothing alarming, heard nothing alarming, with the shore to his right and the lake full of skaters and ice fishermen to his left and the dogs running joyfully behind him— onto the shore, back onto the lake, onto the shore, back onto the lake. But when he stopped for a moment, turned, and called the dogs, only Iggy appeared.

There are tragedies you avoid because you know how to: you wear your seat belt, you don't smoke, you don't take selfies on the edge of a cliff. And then there are the tragedies that you didn't even know to prepare for. Why does a conscientious owner let her dogs run free on an imperfectly frozen lake? By way of explanation, I can only offer a poem from Mary Oliver's wonderful book *Dog Songs:*

> You may not agree, you may not care, but
> if you are holding this book you should know
> that of all the sights I love in this world—
> and there are plenty—very near the top of
> the list is this one: dogs without leashes.

None of the locals who aided in Rebel's search scolded us for not knowing what might happen to a free-roaming puppy on a winter lake. Not Kayla, the lovely young woman working at Price Chopper who helped me copy fifty-five flyers to stuff in neighborhood mailboxes. Not Steve Caporizzo, WABC meteorologist and Albany's patron saint of lost pets, who responded to my Facebook message on New Year's Day within an hour and posted to his seventy thousand followers. Not the woman at the Rite Aid or the one at the Valero station or the one at Main Street Ice Cream Parlor, all of whom reacted sympathetically when I burst into tears in their presence. Not the dog warden or the ASPCA receptionist or even the cashier at McCluskey's Hardware, who told me that she'd never gotten another dog because of exactly what I was going through. She must have known, as I now do, why Louis C.K. referred to getting a puppy as a "countdown to sorrow."

For most of my adult life, whenever I wake up in the middle of the night, my head is filled with worry, mostly about my kids and involving the same well-traveled themes (*Will this one become a drug addict? Will this one ever fall in love?* And more—see chapter 3 for details). I lie awake, letting these dangerous thoughts turn, boring and consistent, rotisserie-style, in my head until eventually I fall asleep again. In the morning, they are gone. During my waking hours, like many people, I worry about things that are easy, nonthreatening, meaningless (*Should I match my socks to my shoes or my pants? How many calories are in one Twizzler?*). I've come to believe that worrying about stupid things is a protective mechanism to keep my days from becoming consumed by the larger, realer, unsolvable worries that visit me at night.

I would never want my days to be filled with *real* worry. I am so blessed that, for much of my life, my days have not been consumed by real worry. But there is something clarifying in the arrival of a real worry, when the quotidian details of your life fall away. Such were my first few days of 2017. Clarifying, in a horrible sort of way.

• • •

Because the lot on which our house is perched is so steep, we were forced to build a ninety-foot wall just below the walkout basement because of somethingsomething-erosionsomething that was patiently explained to me by the builder but seemed too boring to remember. But the wall—long, stone, beautiful—has become quite useful; it's a guardrail, a bench, a balance beam. It separates the relatively flat house-occupying part of our property from the steep unkemptness of what's below it as you make your way down to the lake. After Rebel disappeared, I would stand at the living-room window looking out across the wall to the silent, frozen expanse of lake below, the sun just coming up over the pine trees on the eastern shore. I would look at the lake and hope-imagine I saw a black dot, zigzagging, nose down, making its way toward me. Some days I was sure that if I stared long enough, I really could make that black dot appear.

Once she reached her seventies, my mother—my vibrant, healthy, faculties-totally-intact mother—told me that her very favorite time of day was the few moments after she woke up and before she had to move her body and some part of it (her rotator cuff, her neck, her sciatic nerve) began to hurt. I thought of this in the days after Rebel disappeared, when I could enjoy those first seconds of being awake, lying drowsily under the comforter in my bed, the winter sun pouring onto the lake and through the cracks in my bedroom curtains, when I would forget that Rebel was gone. And then I would remember and drag my body (and my heart, the part that hurt) to the window to try to will the black dot into existence.

The members of my family of five were united in our grief and in the project of finding Rebel. There was only one argument, and that was after I referred to Rebel's disappearance as "a small tragedy." Owen was indignant that I kept using that phrase; in his mind, there was nothing small about the love we had for Rebel, the events of that Saturday, or the way he felt afterward. At age twenty-one, my son was young and lucky enough that he had never fully experienced what I considered "real" tragedy—the death of a friend's child, 9/11. But for him, losing a dog was no small tragedy. His truth, as they say, was his truth. And so I removed the word *small*.

The amount of time people I didn't know were willing to devote to the search for a dog they'd never met was overwhelming, and acknowledging their kind efforts was like standing outside in a snowstorm trying to catch snowflakes on your tongue. You couldn't possibly catch every one, and they just kept coming. In the following days and weeks—and months!—so many strangers called me that I didn't get all of their names.

I was, however, on a first-name basis with Barbara and Christina, two women who progressed from reading Steve Caporizzo's Facebook post to commenting on the post to finding my cell number to texting me with comforting, if astonishing, regularity. It seems there are people in this world who are always on the lookout for a cause, and when they find one, they dive in like teenage boys at a swimming hole, without checking first to see how deep the water is. For Barbara and Christina, I became the cause.

Barbara was encouraging and gentle and a firm believer in the effectiveness of search parties, in part because a search party had provided the happy ending for a black Lab named Otis who was hit by a car and lay for two days incapacitated and undetected in the woods that ran along the road. Barbara offered to drive the two hours from her house to put together a search party for me. When I demurred, she offered again. Barbara also called a friend of hers, a veterinary technician, and had a long talk with him about Rebel's situation. Afterward she called me to relay her friend's opinion, which was that "Labs definitely do not drown."

Christina never called me, which was probably a good thing, because her texts were very...insistent. She insisted I hire a pet tracker, insisted that PackLeader PetTrackers, out of Rhode Island, was the best, and insisted I send a message to the PackLeader owner, Jamie Genereux. I realize now that when you are in a situation that seems hopeless, the people who have made you their cause will insist that all hope is not lost. And they will insist that you not give up. Sometimes the insistence is so overwhelming—and you feel so clueless, confused, and numb—that you do everything they tell you to do.

And so we put up big neon-cardboard signs around town, secured with duct tape to telephone poles and tacked to bulletin boards at Tops and Price Chopper and the Chestertown dump. We stuffed mailboxes all around the lake with flyers detailing Rebel's disappearance. We made a scent trail of kibble from the spot where he disappeared, fried meat on the grill for hours at a time, left our dirty laundry on the front porch. And finally, on day seven, we engaged the services of Jamie Genereux, who drove over from Rhode Island with his dog Dexter (a black Lab—the irony!) in the back of his truck.

Jamie was quite handsome, with blue eyes that matched the color of the January sky and close-shaven facial hair that wasn't a beard but wasn't stubble either. He might have been thirty-five or he might have been fifty. He wore camo overalls and a camo coat and the outfit looked like it had about seventy-five pockets. Incongruously, his hat was pink, with a black Lab stitched on the front. From the passenger side of his truck emerged a young woman whom he introduced, simply, as Bridget. Bridget's long legs were clad in black leggings, and she wore a purple ski parka and a pastel wool hat with a cheery pom-pom on top. She was blond and pretty in a 1980s-movie head-cheerleader sort of way, and because Jamie was thirty-five or fifty, Bridget was maybe his girlfriend or maybe his daughter.

The temperature was in the low twenties and I was wearing ski pants with long johns underneath, a sweater, and a parka; I had hand warmers in my ski mittens and toe warmers in my lined boots. I was demonstrably an amateur and a flatlander, and this feeling—that I was a faux Adirondack resident who didn't know how to dress or hold on to her dog—stuck with me the entire day.

Jamie, Bridget, Owen, and I followed Dexter, start-ing out where we thought Rebel disappeared. I hated being there. I felt angry and sad and incompetent and, most of all, scared at what we might discover. Once we were out on the ice, Jamie walked so quickly that I wondered if he knew the answer to this mystery even before he had been given the full set of clues. Owen and I fell farther and farther behind, watching Jamie with Bridget striding alongside him, wondering what they were talking about. Because Jamie was one of those people who tell you nothing, I of course wanted to know everything. He exhibited no outward signs of emotion—no sorrow or regret about the reason he was there, no frustration that the lake was vast and frozen and the woods were vast and thick and there seemed to be nothing to see. Gloveless, he lit a cigarette from time to time; trailing behind him, I wondered idly whether his smoking interfered with Dexter's sense of smell.

My brother-in-law Gavin once had a yellow Lab named Hazel who went duck hunting with him on the weekends. On days that they didn't hunt, Gavin and Hazel practiced their skills in a little pond near their house; he would launch a duck decoy into the pond and Hazel would leap from the shore with a high arc, like water coming out of a public fountain, dutifully grab the decoy in her jaws, and swim it back to Gavin.

I thought Hazel's performance was almost balletic and I would go on and on about how astounding she was, how athletic, how smart, how loyal, how beautiful. Gavin, however, regarded Hazel with clinical detachment, the same way he viewed his chain saw or his rototiller. Hazel was a tool—the furry kind that would lick his hand and wag her tail, but a tool nonetheless. Growing up, my sisters and I, in an effort to make our dalmatian Pepper one of us, would routinely adorn her with a silk scarf around her neck, a winter hat on her head, and mittens on her front paws, so I was unaccustomed to the notion of a dog who was Not a Pet.

Like Dexter. Jamie followed his dog at a distance; he stopped with him from time to time and said, "Where's the puppy, Dexter? Go get the puppy." He raised his voice only once, when Dexter approached an area of open water near a dock with a bubbler. Then Jamie angrily commanded him to heel. He shook his head disapprovingly at the bubbler and said nothing.

If you live in a part of the world where the winters are harsh, and you build a wooden dock that stays in the water year-round, you are advised to install a bubbler in the winter to keep the water around your dock from freezing and prevent the damage ice may cause.

Our dock is shaped like an L and made of wood. In springtime new dragonflies emerge from the water, crawl up the sides, and fly away. In summertime big dock spiders build webs along the ladders from the water. In the fall, when there is no boat traffic to churn up the silt, you can see clear to the bottom more than eight feet out. And in the winter, to protect our dock, we install a bubbler. I did not share this fact with Jamie. Instead I said, "Someone told me that a Lab wouldn't drown."

"Labs drown all the time," he replied.

In a case like ours, he explained, the dog would continue to try to get back to its handler. If my husband was walking out on the ice and Rebel fell through a patch made thin by a bubbler around a dock, Rebel would keep trying to get to him. His canine instincts would not, in other words, instruct him to sensibly turn around, swim to shore, walk along the shore until the open water near the bubbler became properly frozen ice, and trot out to his human. I absorbed his matter-of-fact explanation like I was studying for a science test. I suddenly realized that Jamie's lack of discernible emotion must be a plus in his line of work. He dealt in facts, not feelings, because his (desperate, bereft) clients had more than enough feelings to go around.

We walked along the lake and up the road, zigzagging through properties and passing empty houses. If given the right prompts, Jamie had all sorts of information to impart. That a Lab outside alone in the Adirondacks would "show up on someone's porch after five days"; that not only do dogs drown but some of them "sink immediately. Depends on the dog"; that it's not just oceans that have currents—lakes have them too; that a Lab "would eat bear shit if it had to" to stay alive and could survive outside in freezing temperatures "indef-initely"; and that there was an easy way to tell coyote tracks from dog tracks: dogs' rear-paw prints appear slightly to the side of their front-paw prints, whereas coyotes' rear-paw prints are directly in line with or on top of their front-paw ones.

We reached a point at about hour three when it seemed like Jamie was going through the motions for my benefit. Maybe he solved the puzzle before he arrived; maybe, when he explained that Dexter kept leading us to the water, he noticed something I failed to see. Maybe because of Christina's texts or because I wanted to believe in a happy ending, I had elevated Jamie, even before he'd arrived, to a status reserved for the obstetrician who delivered my sons. I had blind faith in him. I believed he had powers I lacked, saw things I didn't, could explain mysteries about life and death that I could spend the rest of my days trying to figure out. I wanted Jamie to deliver a dog, or at least deliver an answer. And because of that, I was willing to believe just about anything he told me.

By three p.m. we had walked nearly seven miles on the ice, on snow-packed roads, through woods and fields where we'd sunk up to our shins. We saw dog tracks and deer tracks and coyote tracks and fox tracks, not to mention two empty pizza boxes deep in the woods. Signs of all kinds of life, but no signs of Rebel. We returned to the house, and as we stood in our mudroom saying goodbye, Iggy wriggled to sit between Jamie's legs. And it was then—when Jamie's face finally broke into a wide smile and he reached down to scratch Iggy's ears—that I knew he recognized the difference between a tool and a pet.

Before Jamie climbed back into his truck, I asked

him, "If this were your dog, what would you think happened to it?"

His reply was immediate. "If this were my dog," he said, "I would think he drowned."

• • •

After Rebel disappeared I read a number of books, both fiction and nonfiction, about dogs. I was struck by this passage in Alexandra Horowitz's *Inside of a Dog,* in which she talks about her dog Pumpernickel:

More than once Pumpernickel got herself in dire straits (once, trapped on a catwalk heading off a building edge; another time, her leash stuck in the elevator doors as the car began to move). I was amazed at how unfazed she appeared— especially as contrasted with my own alarm. It was never she who got herself out of the fix. I believe that I was more worried about her well-being than she was about mine. Still, much of my well-being hinged on her—not on her knowing how to fix dilemmas, great or small, in my life, but rather on her unremitting cheer and constant companionship.

By the late fall of 2016—after my career had fizzled, after Hugo had gone off to college and contracted Lyme disease, after Trump was elected—I had come to count on Rebel's cheer and companionship as a daily balm. When he greeted me at the front door with his silly felt toy in his mouth, my heart swelled. Happiness is concentric and whole, as colorful and perfect as a soap bubble. But right before a soap bubble pops you can see, in the swirling colors, the thin place emerging. The beginnings of the pop, before the pop. In the fall of 2016, my bubble was already thinning. For days and weeks after Rebel disappeared at the end of December, I kept replaying the final minutes that he was present and visible in our lives. On that cold Saturday when the bubble finally popped, when the visible became invisible, it happened silently. Didn't he know how much I needed him?

Eventually the normal routines of life had to return. Winter break ended; my husband went back to work and my children went back to school. Rebel did not turn up, and the jagged pain of not knowing where he was became smoother over time. As the weeks passed, there were little eruptions of hope—in January, over Martin Luther King Jr. weekend, I received a flurry of calls from neighbors who saw a black Lab wearing a red collar and limping, wandering around the lake.

Maybe he was wearing a harness collar. Maybe the collar wasn't red at all—maybe it was orange. One woman contacted me because her security camera had picked up an image of a dog eating corn she'd left out in her yard. She sent me a screenshot. Was that dog Rebel? My husband sat at his desk, with me looking over his shoulder, and enlarged the photo so we could see more. It just got bigger, not clearer. Like the story itself.

Some years death feels like an abstract concept; some years it feels like a faraway destination; and some years it feels like background music. In the months following Rebel's disappearance, the background music got louder: In the summer of 2017, both Owen and Hugo were involved in serious car accidents that left their cars totaled but their bodies intact, if shaken. Owen graduated from college and, several weeks later, attended the funeral of his college roommate.

The tragedy of Rebel began to feel less immediate. When I drove to the Adirondacks I imagined I was a shiny, perfect apple with a bruised spot no one could see. Even I forgot about the bruised spot, but then, as I got closer to our house, winding along Route 28, the Hudson River flowing past the driver's side window, I hit the bruised spot, and something invisible hurt. From time to time I would get a call, and one day in March I saw a quartet of eagles tearing something apart on the surface of the frozen lake, and I worried it was the body of a drowned dog until my binoculars convinced me it wasn't. I will never forget the sight of those giant birds, a ferocious reminder that when I am inside my house next to the fireplace, watching a movie on my big TV with a cup of tea in my hand— well, I am living in an alternate Adirondack universe. The real Adirondacks are outside the window, and they are enormous and unknowable and wild.

And then, on a beautiful Saturday night at the very end of June, six months after we last saw our puppy, the phone rang. I was at home in Westchester County and I ignored the call, which came from an unfamiliar number. It was dinnertime, and all the boys were home, and the weather was beautiful as we sat in the twilight on the patio. Seconds later, Valerie sent me a text: *Call me. They found Rebel.*

His body had come to rest on the shore of the lake, close to the spot where he had disappeared. I was four hours away, and a man I had never met pulled his body from the water. A woman I didn't know put it in a bag, first removing his collar and cleaning his tags for us to keep. When I phoned to thank her later she told me that "good goes around and around and around, and whether it's a stranger or a close friend, when you have the opportunity to do something kind, you do it." Another stranger buried Rebel on our property, on a ridge overlooking our house, overlooking the lake. When I tried to pay him he said, "I am not comfortable taking money for something like this." I did not ask for these kindnesses. They just came to me, and I tried to hold on to them. Snowflakes melting on my tongue.

In an obituary for his dog Daisy, E. B. White wrote, "She never grew up, and she never took pains to discover, conclusively, the things that might have diminished her curiosity and spoiled her taste. She died sniffing life, and enjoying it." Rebel never grew up and died doing something he loved: chasing Iggy around the lake.

A guide dog is bred and trained to broaden the world for a visually impaired partner—to be the human's eyes, to make his or her journey through life easier and better. Rebel didn't have the drive or intelligence or discipline to provide years of support to a blind partner. But he did broaden my world. Our house on the little Adirondack lake had been a snug family refuge, two blond sisters in their own private canoe, until it became the fulcrum in an operation of community spirit. Someone once told me that a family must live in the Adirondacks for at least three generations before anyone in it can be considered a native. I will never achieve that status, and apparently neither will my children. But I like to think that, in the public show of concern and sadness that followed the death of Rebel, this flatlander took a little shortcut to belonging.

Late one afternoon this past summer I kayaked north on the lake, passing the spot where Rebel was found. I felt a wave of melancholy that was sudden but not altogether unpleasant, like when you are swimming in the lake and move through a pocket of warm water. On my way back south toward our house, I stopped to chat with a couple sitting on their dock. They introduced themselves, and I recognized their last name; they were the brother and sister-in-law of a man who had e-mailed me frequently in the days after Rebel disappeared. And so I said, "I am the woman whose dog drowned." Then their eyes softened, because—of course—they'd heard of me, and they shared their own story, how their elderly Lab had died the previous winter. I will always be known on the lake as the woman who lost her dog. Which is both embarrassing and sad. But that identity brings something else too: strangers who are no longer strangers, everywhere I look.

Chapter 12

Iris, Karl, the Bathing Ape, and Me

"Mom made the cut." That's what the bouncer said, and although my brain knew that these words should not matter, my heart felt a little thrill as he ushered me, Laura, and Axel into the store. We had been standing outside for forty minutes in ninety-degree heat, surrounded by people I didn't understand, waiting to get into a store I'd never heard of. The white cutoff-jean shorts and Birkenstocks I wore—while fine for my normal suburban life—were the equivalent of a neon sign flashing on my ass that said YES, THAT'S RIGHT, I'M A TOURIST. So when the bouncer from Black Tie Professional Services told me I was worthy, I felt a gratitude that nearly brought me to tears.

I'd lived in New York for thirty-two years, spending my days on the Upper West Side, in Midtown East, Midtown West, the financial district, and Brooklyn. I'd worked at *Vogue* and *Glamour,* attended crowded, chaotic fashion shows and crowded, chaotic sample sales. I had a number of friends (and even a sister) who worked in clothing retail. Suffice it to say that when it came to fashion, I hadn't gotten off the plane from Schiphol yesterday.

But my teenage cousin Laura had—well, seven days before, to be precise—and in the week she'd been with us, something had dawned on me. Laura hadn't come to New York to see me or my kids or my dogs or the Brooklyn Bridge or the Metropolitan Museum of Art or *The Taming of the Shrew* at the Hudson Valley Shakespeare Festival. No, the primary reason Laura had come to visit was so she could stand on Greene Street for the better part of an hour and then overpay for a T-shirt that she would, more likely than not, sell to someone else.

It's not like Laura hadn't prepared me. When Axel and I picked her up at Kennedy Airport, my son watched her approach and said, with wonder, "Mom! She's wearing Yeezys!"

"No she is not," I whispered, although I didn't really know what Yeezys were and was pretty convinced that Axel, who was eleven, didn't either. Once Laura reached us, she gave out quick hugs and announced brightly, and in perfect English, "I would like to go to Chick-Fil-A, Chipotle, and BAPE."

For the record, those *were* Yeezys—the Kanye West mesh sneakers that look like they'd fall apart if you stepped in a shallow puddle and can be yours for a mere four hundred dollars—on her feet. One of two pairs she owned. She used to have more but she sold them, for double her purchase price, which was how she could afford the Gucci tennis shoes and Hermès belt that she brought with her on the trip to America. As far as I knew, Laura was not rich, although it's hard to tell with those Europeans. It wasn't like she lived in a castle or anything. I think she was just canny and perhaps, although she might not know the term, what my kids called a "hype beast." My husband and I happened to be in Amsterdam and had had dinner with Laura and her family a few months before her trip to New York. She sat at the table surrounded by adults talking about private equity and Trump and all manner of topics that left me with the feeling that not only was she more sophisticated than my children, but compared to members of the American side of the family, she was just... what's the word?... *better.*

When we arrived at the BAPE store it was four p.m. and the line to get in stretched from midblock all the way to the corner. As we approached, I thought Laura's resolve might vanish, leaving her crumpled in a little humid ball. "There must have been a drop," she said, crestfallen.

"A what?" I asked.

"Or an Adidas collab," she continued. For a minute it looked like she might cry, although Laura wasn't the crying type. She was smart enough to know that Axel and I didn't want to wait in the heat to get into a store that she alone cared about and gracious enough to announce, with great solemnity, "I think we should go home." But the Tokyo-based BAPE has a limited number of retail stores and I'm not a complete monster. So we waited, me silently trying to figure out exactly when I had stopped understanding fashion and Axel noisily trying to chew a hole in the bottom of a plastic water bottle, sweat trickling down his little blond sideburns.

Maybe when you are a teenager in Europe, you just know certain things. The weather during Laura's July stay had been relentlessly hot and humid, and one morning she walked out of the front door, threw her hands in the air, and proclaimed, "It feels like Vietnam!" Which is not something any American kid I know would ever think, much less proclaim on the porch. One summer we swapped houses with Laura and her family, and after a week at our place, her mother was agog at how chic she thought New York women were. I suppose that is objectively true. And I suppose, objectively speaking, that I am a New York woman. But standing there on Greene Street, I was reminded that it was the Dutch who settled Manhattan. And almost four centuries later, sixteen-year-old Laura had swept into town to obliterate what little cool I still possessed.

• • •

A woman is like a swallowtail butterfly: When she is young she is a gorgeous caterpillar, enchanting and graceful. In the middle of her life she disappears into her cocoon. The cocoon phase is long; the woman is hidden, all but invisible to the world, unremarkable. But when she gets to be eighty-five—if she gets to be eighty-five—she emerges from her cocoon more beautiful and amazing than anyone could have predicted. Her looks and dignity are more clearly defined than ever. And if she lasts another ten years, she gets a modeling contract and a Barbie created in her likeness. In other words, she becomes Iris Apfel.

These days, everyone wants to grow up to be Iris Apfel. Maybe the name means nothing to you, but you've seen her: enormous round black glasses, a head of thick white hair in a cheerful cropped style, high collars, colorful scarves, loads of big necklaces, giant rings on every finger, cuffs everywhere. To call someone an old woman seems like an insult. But Iris is, at this writing, ninety-nine. She is, unequivocally, an old woman. If Iris Apfel were sixty-nine, she would be neither an old woman nor the celebrity that she is, someone still out in the world, lugging around all that jewelry, smiling behind the black glasses, getting a Barbie doll named after her. She even has a contract with IMG, the modeling agency that represents Gigi Hadid and Karlie Kloss.

At this point I do feel compelled to mention that Iris Apfel has no children, which explains almost everything.

I know people who have met Iris Apfel, and apparently she is as wonderful as she looks. Still, do you really want to be her? Here are your choices if you are lucky (or unlucky) enough to live to ninety-nine: you can devote most of your waking hours to hair, makeup, and chunky turquoise necklaces, or you can spend your days puttering around in a garden someplace, wearing jeans that are thirty years old, not caring that there's dirt under your fingernails, humming songs you only partially remember and yelling obscenities at no one in particular. It's possible you will have a thick head of hair like Iris Apfel but more likely you will have eight stringy strands left on your scalp, and they will hang down your back like the sad pieces of angel hair pasta someone left stuck to the bottom of the pan after everyone served themselves.

A woman reaches a point in her relationship to fashion when she has to either buckle down or give up. This, apparently, is where I am now. Staying modern has become a fight, and I'm not sure the fight is worth it. There was a time when fashion mattered to me, because my job depended on it. When I started at *Vogue*, at the age of twenty-seven, I worked in the features department, meaning I was not one of the fashion editors, the ones who really understood, absorbed, and then dictated to the masses whatever it was designers were trying to communicate. I was on the periphery, but I knew that fashion advertising paid my salary, so I forced myself to learn.

I never made it to the best sample sales—the really good ones were invitation-only—but I got around that by driving up the New York State Thruway to the Woodbury Common outlets and buying last season's Prada pants. Did that make me feel like a lemming? Yes. Was that why I had gone to graduate school? No. But I wanted to succeed at work and a lemming trek to buy Prada at a discount wasn't unethical, illegal, or dangerous. When you are twenty-seven and making twenty-six thousand dollars a year, you do what you must to demonstrate to the boss that you're trying as hard as you can.

While I was at *Vogue,* a well-known editor (the sort who made the magic happen with photographers and models on beaches and at villas in countries I couldn't even spell) was pregnant at the same time I was. She was impossibly skinny, a fashion-department greyhound, fast and slippery, while I was a features-department St. Bernard, solid and dependable. One day she appeared in my office with the news that her obstetrician had told her she needed to eat more protein and she thought I might know how to do that.

"Eggs have protein," I said. She blinked at me. "And chicken."

"Oh," she said, her face alive with wonderment.

"Beef has protein?" I said, waiting to see some light bulb, however dim, appear over her head.

This went on and on. The woman's ignorance

about food was spectacular. Was I being played? Was she a heroin addict? Were we even living in the same dimension? Who's to say? All I know is that she could wear a bikini top to the office and pull it off, which she did one day. She stood at the fax machine half naked, and I watched her for a minute from down the hall, stupefied. You can learn that a ham sandwich has protein, but knowing how to pull off a bikini top in the office? That's something that can't be taught.

I remained a breed apart, always keeping one foot in the practical world of my upbringing, where my mother sewed my parochial-school skirts on an old Singer in the laundry room and taught me that pretty is as pretty does. For the magazine's hundredth-anniversary party—which was held at the New York Public Library on Fifth Avenue—I pulled out of my closet a black silk dress with crisscross straps in the back and a matching diaphanous shawl, an outfit my mother had made for me to wear to a sorority formal when I was a sophomore in college. It was a beautiful dress, my mom's Newark, Delaware, rendition of haute couture, and I still have it. I know where my loyalties lie.

At the *Vogue* party there was music and dancing in the library's vast entrance hall, but a fellow assistant and I stood leaning against a marble column, too self-conscious to join the supermodels and designers and extremely rich people crowding the floor. After all, I had on a homemade dress and the people surrounding me were wearing outfits that cost nearly as much as my annual salary. A kind editor in her forties came up behind me and gave me a gentle shove. "Get out there," she said.

"Why?"

"Because the older people like to watch you young women having fun."

Karl Lagerfeld—who was at that *Vogue* party—died in 2019, but before he did, he said a lot of memorable things, including this: "Sweatpants are a sign of defeat. You lost control of your life so you bought some sweatpants." And this: "Vanity is the healthiest thing in life." It's been decades since my *Vogue* job; I haven't been to Woodbury Common in years, and I have gone back to believing that an obsession with fashion is frivolous, and vanity is not only *not* healthy, but a trap.

Sometimes now I will wear something cool, but it's always by accident. Last month there was an article in the *New York Times* about a brand of clogs I have been loyal to for more than a decade, since the day I was at a photo shoot and watched the food stylist clip-clop around the set in them, all badass determination and vitality. When I asked about her clogs, she told me that they were from a store in SoHo, she could stand in them all day and her feet never hurt, and they were waterproof. Trifecta! I now own three pairs— black, brown, and gray. As far as clogs go, they are stupidly expensive, but they last forever, so the price-per-wear amortization makes them worth every cent. Now, apparently, "my" clogs have become some sort of coolness signifier for middle-aged Brooklyn moms. For the record, the article noted that in addition to the clogs, the truly cool mom must have hooked to her bag a colorful, detachable purse strap that costs $140 (purse not included!), and, while it's interesting-looking, you'd need to have your head examined if you spent that much money on a *strap*. The day the article appeared, I happened to be wearing the suddenly-cool-in-Brooklyn clogs to work, and a colleague who had seen the story asked me about them. I felt a curious combination of pride (I was current!) and shame (the article mentioned the price of the clogs). Of course, the Brooklyn moms will quickly move on to other footwear while I will continue to wear my clogs for another twenty years with a practicality that would make my mother proud but that will never be covered in the *New York Times*.

There is no death knell that chimes the moment you stop knowing how to dress. But it comes, silently, for all of us who aren't that skinny protein-deprived editor or Iris Apfel. It has something to do with not paying attention and something to do with not caring and something to do with too many candles on your birthday cake. And it wasn't until I found myself on Greene Street with Laura that I knew the bell had tolled for me.

• • •

My mother once told me, "After you get to be a certain age, everyone under twenty-five is beautiful." She was absolutely right about that, and my cousin Laura was beautiful, both objectively and because she was only sixteen. I observed her as we stood in line; she waited patiently, uncrumpled, unruffled, making effortless conversation with the man in front of us. His name was Kevin and he was visiting from Los Angeles and he understood things about Laura that I didn't—they spoke in a fashion lingua franca that remained out of my reach. In an attempt to make this sweaty, boring experience a teachable moment, I turned to Axel and tried to explain how, in retail, scarcity can increase demand; after seven seconds he could tell that the conversation was not going to lead to Fortnite and he stopped listening. Next to the long sidewalk line there was a weird, shorter line, which had apparently started at 7:30 a.m.

and was populated by furtive-looking people wearing wristbands. I never figured out who they were, but their line moved faster than ours and when they went in, they sprinted up the stairs and came out five minutes later. I think this had something to do with the *drop* and the *collab,* but I never got to the bottom of it.

And then we reached the front of the line and the bouncer, who had been eyeing my outfit with horror, said those most exciting words—"Mom made the cut"—and ushered us inside.

How do you say "Not worth the long hot wait with Kevin" in Japanese? The store itself was essentially one long corridor with hidden doors that sweat-suit-clad people (paging Karl Lagerfeld!) who might have been employees or might have been shoppers kept slipping into. A silent intensity blanketed the room as the lucky few standing inside scrutinized what inventory remained. The merchandise at BAPE—or Bathing Ape, as it is called by no one—has two themes: shark teeth and camouflage. This nonsensical combination was familiar to me because on the night Laura arrived at my house, we had looked together at the BAPE website. Where she saw the promised land, I saw sad models wearing clothes that didn't fit. Staring at the computer screen, I asked Laura whether her mother liked BAPE, and she laughed.

"How old is she?" I asked.

"She is *so old*," she said. "Fifty-four."

I told her that I was also fifty-four.

Now that I was inside the store, I understood BAPE even less. For about thirty seconds, I combed through the racks to see if there was anything for me to buy. The women's sizes started at small and went down (yes, down) from there. The prices were what you would expect when you enter only a handful of stores in the whole world after waiting forty minutes to get inside: a T-shirt was over one hundred dollars. I stepped back from the rack and looked down at my white cutoff jeans and red Birkenstocks, which signified that I was not Iris Apfel or a fashion editor or a BAPE regular but just your average suburban mom. I didn't want to be a BAPE shopper. I didn't want to be chasing cool. I didn't want to understand what about this store excited Laura and Kevin and everyone else. I just wanted to go home. Which is not to say I didn't pull out my wallet; I had promised that I would try to find something for Axel to reward his stoicism in the face of extreme retail boredom. And so I got him a hat, but as I handed it to him I hissed, "You are never allowed to tell any of your friends how much this cost."

As we were leaving, Kevin stopped Laura to ask her opinion about a jacket; she gave it to him with the quiet authority of a sixteen-year-old who understands things like private equity and just how humid it is in Vietnam. In the end there wasn't much for Laura to buy, which she accepted with equanimity. She did get a shirt, an ugly T-shirt that didn't really fit, in my humble fifty-four-year-old opinion. After Laura returned to Holland, I saw that she posted a picture of herself wearing it on Instagram, but only once. She probably sold it and made a nice little profit.

Chapter 13

What We Talk About
When We Talk About
Love

Kristin's Marriage Compatibility Test:

- Toilet paper: Roll from top or from bottom?
- If you don't take your shoes off when you enter the house, will you sweep up the little crusts of dirt that fall from the treads? Related question: Do you even notice when the floor is dirty?

- Your mother and your spouse disagree. Do you take a side? If so, whose?
- Your spouse announces that she wants to change her hairstyle / the sofa pillows / her job / you. Now are you paying attention?
- You can't find your house key. Whose fault is that?
- The dog obviously loves your spouse more. Does that make you mad?
- Kids may ruin your relationship. Should you have them?
- Your spouse says, "Will you do me a favor?" Is your response (a) "Sure!" or (b) "What is it?"
- Broccoli for dinner: Steamed or roasted?
- How do you feel about the movie *What's Up, Doc?*

• • •

It was a magazine ad for De Beers diamonds, featuring an attractive couple—heterosexual, of course, because this was the 1970s—lying together on a beach. The man is wearing a fisherman's sweater and has curly hair very much like Christopher Atkins (who was, at the time, my imaginary and only boyfriend) in the movie *The Blue Lagoon*. The woman has flowing brown hair and a serene face and rests her head on his chest. Their eyes are closed in order to communicate how very much in love they are and to allow the reader's attention to focus immediately on the diamond solitaire the woman wears. The lone line of copy is this: *Sometimes we talk for hours and never say a word.*

If you don't remember the ad, maybe it didn't wreck your understanding of relationships for most of your teens. But that's certainly the effect it had on me. Because, to my teenage brain (and heart!), this was the. Height. Of. Romance.

Forget "Love means never having to say you're sorry." (And more on Ryan O'Neal in a minute.) True, deep, lasting love meant never having to say anything at all. When you found your soul mate, communication was fluid and silent and telepathic... or something. The practical details didn't matter! All I knew was that when I found my Christopher Atkins / De Beers guy soul mate, a whole rich world would open up before me, one that involved wordless conversations and sex in a claw-foot tub.

Which is exactly how my life has turned out.

JK! Now that forty years have passed, I see the ad differently, and not just because I need magnification to make out the copy. First, lying on the beach without a blanket just means a lot of sand in your hair. Like bubble gum, sand is impossible to get out of your hair unless you're willing to accept that by the time you're done you'll be six months older. Shirley Conran famously said that life's too short to stuff a mushroom. I'd rather stuff a hundred mushrooms using needle-nose pliers than try to get sand out of my hair. Second, the guy in the ad is wearing a heavy, warm-looking, long-sleeved sweater while the woman wears only a short-sleeved cotton shirt. Isn't she cold? As he was putting on his thick, cozy sweater, did he think to ask her whether she too might need another layer? Fat chance. Just like all the fathers who think that pre-paring for vacation means packing only for themselves while the children's suitcases get packed by magic elves, Mr. Sand in Hair wasn't thinking about his fiancée's bare arms. If the situation were reversed, no doubt she would have said to him, "It looks chilly—do you want to bring your sweater?" Or she would have just shoved the giant sweater into her purse, next to the Purell, Neosporin, Advil, and travel-size tissues that someone somewhere someday might need.

Finally, the talking-without-saying-anything thing. My husband and I have been married for twenty-nine years and we still haven't mastered telepathic commu-nication. When we are together for hours not saying a word, it means that we are either mad at each other or in the car listening to a podcast. Which he likes to play on 1.5x speed, which makes me feel like I am about to have a heart attack. Life is fast enough already without having to hear Men in Blazers talk about Everton like they've just sucked on a helium balloon.

On the occasions when we do talk for hours—out loud, like your average unremarkable couple who'd never appear in an ad—it's about things like whether any of our kids will ever amount to anything or if it's worth paying the extra money to book a flight that doesn't have a five-hour layover in Dallas.

• • •

My father is a fairly predictable man who is rarely at a loss for words. There are a few expressions and statements that come out of his mouth so often, they've nearly become family slogans. Every meal he's ever eaten has been "really very good"; every cold he gets—and he gets a lot of colds—is a "terrible cold." If he's ever had an ordinary meal or a mild cold, we haven't heard about it. When he wants to help himself to more ice cream he says, "I guess I'd better have another shot," and when he sinks the wrong ball while playing pool with a grandchild he will exclaim, "Piet, you donkey!" Drive through a neighborhood full of enormous houses with my father and he'll say, "There's a paucity of poor folks around here." The fact that all of us have heard him utter these things dozens of times is not so much annoying or tedious as strangely comforting. A bit of order in a disordered world.

Dad believes in love and in the traditions it involves. Once he knew my then-boyfriend and I were serious about each other, one of my father's stock statements to him became "Assuming you marry my daughter—and we can assume that, can't we?" He is constantly talking to himself or to my mother or to someone else about my mother. When Mom irritates him, he will turn to me and my sisters and say, "Girls, I really love your mother, but..." My parents have been married for fifty-eight years. If it's first thing in the morning and you and Dad are in the living room and Mom comes out of the bedroom, he will turn to you and say, "Now, who's this beauty walking down the stairs?" She will go to him and he will put his arms around her and give her a kiss on the cheek.

My father has opinions on everything, from world politics to how to open a box of cereal from Trader Joe's. And yet when I e-mailed to ask him the secret to a long marriage, he never responded. I don't quite understand why. But I also haven't pressed him on it. And I don't understand that either.

• • •

I started dating the man I eventually married when I was a senior in college. We were introduced by my roommate, Mary Lewis, and her boyfriend, Dan. After graduation, we all moved to Washington, DC, where Mary Lewis and I lived on MacArthur Boulevard across from a liquor store run by a friendly man who, when he learned I was from Delaware, taught me this: "If Mississippi and Missouri got a New Jersey, what would Delaware?"

One night my parents and sisters came to visit and we all watched the movie *What's Up, Doc?* sprawled on the floor of the little living room in that second-story MacArthur Boulevard apartment. *What's Up, Doc?* was the van Ogtrop litmus test for admittance to the tribe. If you didn't think *What's Up, Doc?* was one of the best movies ever made, then you were not permitted to join.

My boyfriend laughed in all the right places that night, and he sailed through the family approval process. Still, his devotion to the movie has never matched mine, which is a lingering disappointment. I could write a whole book about how much I love *What's Up, Doc?* The first chapter would be called "Howard Bannister: I Challenge You to Find a Better Fictional Name." We won't get into my complete thoughts on the movie, but I must mention the scene in which Howard has just begun to demonstrate to his fiancée, Eunice, by his inattentiveness and goofy, clueless nature that he might not be the go-to guy for the long term. Eunice is getting him dressed for his big career-making dinner, helping hapless Howard tie his tie, and their conversation goes like this:

> Eunice: I'm not looking for romance, Howard.
> Howard: Oh?
> Eunice: No, I'm looking for something more important than that, something stronger. As the years go by, romance fades and something else takes its place. Do you know what that is?
> Howard: Senility?
> Eunice: Trust!
> Howard: That's what I meant.

There are many objectionable things about Eunice, who is played by Madeline Kahn with a spectacular, simmering fury. She is shrewish and condescending and jumps up on the bed screeching like a monkey when she thinks there is a snake in her hotel room. She has naturally red hair that looks pretty and thick and yet she wears a red-haired wig. I ask you: What's the point of that? And Eunice is wrong in her insistence that trust takes the place of romance. Trust and romance exist symbiotically, rising and falling and completely dependent on each other like kids on a playground seesaw.

In *What's Up, Doc?* Barbra Streisand plays Judy, and Judy never stops talking while Howard (Ryan O'Neal, looking a lot like the De Beers guy) just stares at her with confusion, exasperation, and wonder. What Judy knows immediately but Howard doesn't realize until later is that their courtship is one long inside joke. That's the best part of an intimate relationship: the inside-joke-ness of it all. I sometimes think the primary reason my husband and I stay married is the three decades of inside jokes we've accumulated— that's too much of an investment to abandon. Most of our life together has been spent in our little suburban town, and we have used our imaginations to fill it with a private, custom collection of weirdos who bring a spark of difference to the travel soccer and stainless-steel appliances and privet hedges, those signifiers of belonging and sameness that dull our little corner of America. For example: There is an oddball man on our commuter train whom we refer to as the Explorer because of the way he dresses and the way he walks and the things he carries with him into New York City. We spend a fair amount of time charting the comings and goings of the Explorer; one day last summer I saw him jogging, shirtless, and describing to my husband what that looked like was so exciting, it was as if a peacock had flown through the kitchen window and dropped a gold brick on the counter. The Explorer—a man whose name I don't know and hope never to learn—has no idea what an important role he plays in my marriage. And if I should die first, I'd like my funeral to resemble the court scene in *What's Up, Doc?*, with our ragtag assembly of local inside-joke weirdos—Running Lady, the Dork, Shrek, Perfect Family, Crystal Meth People, Stinky Feet Man, Kronk, Not Fancy Pantsy, and the Explorer—flanking my husband as they watch my casket sink into the ground.

• • •

I got married on a rainy day in June. Multiple people remarked that rain on a wedding day means good luck, which I thought was just hogwash intended to make a bride feel better. Still, I have been married for so long that perhaps it's true. We had a conventional church wedding and, at our reception, a whole roasted pig, tomato aspic, and a vanilla polka-dotted cake with raspberry filling between the layers. There was a steel-drum band, because Dad is from Aruba and just about anybody can dance to steel-drum music. I wore my mother's wedding dress, which we had had altered substantially; it ripped just a bit during the ceremony, and Mom and I found a needle and thread at the reception to make a quick repair before I joined the party. My husband wore a rented white dinner jacket and forgot to remove the tag stapled to the outside of his sleeve, an oversight that was pointed out to him by a groomsman as we stood on the steps of the church after the ceremony, when it was too late for me to change my mind.

When we arrived at our hotel later that night, I realized that I had forgotten my toothbrush. We were so exhausted. I asked the guy at the front desk, "Are most newlyweds this tired when they check in?"

"No," he said flatly.

There were mishaps but no disasters and we ended the whole thing happy and a bit wrung out, which was a fitting preview of our future life together.

When we got married, I was twenty-seven and my husband was twenty-eight and we had been dating for six years. Why did we do it? Even now I'm not entirely sure. Because we were conventional and many of our peers were doing it? Two of our three children have nearly reached the age that we were then, and they seem so *unformed,* I wonder how we knew that a lifetime commitment was a good idea.

• • •

My husband is the Howard to my Judy. Unlike me, he does not feel the need to fill long silences with talking or to share the particulars of his life with everyone in the world in order to make sense of things and feel that he is part of something larger than himself. He prefers to remain unknown—even, sometimes, to me. I hope to be married to him until one of us departs this world, and whether I am standing beside his deathbed or he is standing beside mine, it's possible I will be wondering, *After all these years, do I really know you?* Which partly explains how we stay married. He is a puzzle that I'm still trying to solve.

Whenever I go to a new restaurant or an interesting hotel or a cool building with remarkable architecture without my husband, I wish he were there beside me. I don't know why I feel that way. My mother once told me that too often I am drawn to shallow, insincere, entertainment-value people. People who would never remember how many children I have or the name of the town where I live but who make going out to lunch feel like watching a hilarious or dramatic movie. The man I married is not like that; he is quiet. And he sleeps too late! Over the past three decades I have spent many mornings waiting for him to get out of bed so the day can begin. This is particularly a problem on vacation. But he is the person I want to experience things with.

Is that love? Or is it habit, just where my brain goes, like a set of marble steps that's worn away in the middle because millions of feet have come to rest precisely in the same spot for so many years? And does it even matter?

He is deliberate where I am impatient; methodical where I am hasty; sensitive where I am boorish. He understands the English Premier League and the Middle East, and I know what to wear to a funeral and how to make pasta puttanesca without consulting a recipe. He examines every situation from all sides, which is wonderful, except when it's already six thirty and you haven't figured out what to have for dinner. In the language of decision-making, he is a maximizer and I am a satisficer. Which, I suppose, makes it all the more remarkable that he chose to marry me.

• • •

Sometimes I think loons provide the perfect metaphor for a long marriage. They paddle along, side by side, on the surface of the water; periodically one will dive and the other follows. When they reemerge, often they are side by side again. But sometimes they surface twenty yards apart, and that's when I imagine they are having a fight. Beneath the surface, one of them has said, "You are not the bird I married!"

In *Olive, Again,* Elizabeth Strout's sequel to *Olive Kitteridge,* there is a passage in which Olive contemplates her long marriage to Henry, whom she seems to love and loathe in equal measure. Olive imagines a wall that has come up between them during the course of their relationship; at first it is a pretty, low stone wall but eventually it becomes a giant thing, impermeable and too tall to scale. It has separated them completely.

A few months ago I accompanied my husband to a doctor's appointment. The waiting room was cramped, which meant we were nearly touching knees with an elderly couple sitting across from us. The air around the couple seemed charged; their silences were broken only by little moments of griping at each other. Do we all just get crankier as we get older? I ask myself this nearly every day. Maybe the couple was scared or grieving, and that was the subtext of their exchanges. Maybe they were both in chronic physical pain. Or maybe they were Olive and Henry, and the wall between them was so high that they couldn't ever see the person on the other side.

A nurse appeared at the doorway to the examination rooms and called out a name. With some effort, the man pushed himself up from his chair and shuffled away, still wearing his winter coat over his stooped shoulders, the scowling wife behind him. I looked at my husband and

229

raised my eyebrows just slightly, sensing an inside joke in the making.

Five minutes later they were back. "I told you she said *Johnson!*" the woman hissed as they settled into their seats.

"She said *Paulson,*" he replied. "I'm sure of it."

"You're wrong!" the woman said, rage in her voice. "She was calling someone named Johnson. I told you it wasn't your turn, but you went in anyway!" I did not look over at my husband; these people weren't funny anymore. What was the real problem? Maybe once you are old it becomes very important to be right about dumb little things (Johnson or Paulson) because getting the bigger things wrong (what is shampoo for? do car keys go in the fridge?) is a truly horrifying sign. But, oh my, that couple. Did they ever share words of tenderness?

Yesterday morning I asked my husband to do something that I didn't feel like handling but also didn't have time to do before work. He did not like the way I asked, which was probably passive-aggressively, and he became annoyed. So I said, "That's a dumb thing to be mad at me about," which is itself a dumb thing to say since, as my mother always told me, feelings are neither right nor wrong, they're just there. Who am I to tell him what he can and can't feel? But it just came out of my mouth, like snakes. Then, frowning, he and I went our separate ways for the day.

As I walked to the train I thought, *What if he gets hit by a bus and the very last thing I ever said to him was "That's a dumb thing to be mad at me about"?*

You reach a certain point in middle age when it finally dawns on you that you get only one body, so you'd better protect it. Don't make any risky maneuvers that could threaten the whole enterprise. The same is true for a marriage—you must protect it. Which often means choosing not to fight. Oh, the arguments we used to have when we were younger! We were two sharp rocks in a rock tumbler, flying around in the dark, each hoping to blast the other to pieces. The stakes always seemed high and winning seemed so important. We didn't realize that what was actually happening was that the edges were growing smoother over time.

When we left the doctor's office, I couldn't get the angry couple out of my mind. "Is that just what happens?" I asked my husband as we walked out. "The older you get, the more you hate each other?"

"Not all old couples are like that."

"Promise me," I said fiercely. "Promise me that we will never fight about stupid shit when we're old."

"We won't," he said.

Is divorce unthinkable? Of course not. If you have

been married for longer than six months and divorce has never occurred to you, then either you have no imagination or you are lying to yourself. Divorce is always there, waving at you from the back of the room. People say it's impossible to hold two opposing ideas in your head at the same time, but any married person knows that you can love your spouse and hate him too. There are things about my husband's personality that I didn't like when we were thirty and that I like even less now; when you are in a long marriage, certain traits become distilled, like a sauce that has been reduced on the burner. But divorce would make my life worse, not better. Perhaps I got married because many of my peers were doing it, and it was contagious. I can't say the same about divorce. I've never watched the dissolution of a friend's marriage and thought, *Well! Maybe I should give that a whirl.* Some marriages fade and some explode and some fall victim to a surprise attack like sniper fire from a nearby roof. We endeavor to protect our relationships from destruction, but sometimes we can't. Like most couples, we have had our challenges. But my husband knows that, even when I'm angry or fed up and don't feel like fighting for him, I will always fight for the marriage.

• • •

Mary Lewis and Dan were both in our wedding, and they got—and stayed—married too. Recently their grown daughter asked Mary Lewis what makes a successful marriage, and Mary Lewis posed the question to me. I answered that marriage is a choice you make every single day—whether the thing you don't agree on is worth going to the mat for, whether you still like who you are with your spouse, whether you want this particular person copiloting your plane as it begins its descent. Every day you wake up and you make those choices all over again.

My husband has vetted this essay, of course, because a good spouse does not give away the parts of you that you don't want the world to see. He trusts me, and I trust him. He understands that I am naive and gullible and quick to believe almost anything anybody tells me. He protects me in a world of con artists and liars. Although most lies are small and harmless, everyone lies a little. My husband is the only person in my life who never lies to me. I trust everything he says. And that, Eunice, *is* romance.

When you are sixteen and obsessed with a De Beers ad, you think that what you want from love is an epic, showstopping affair. Little is showstopping about our marriage after twenty-nine years, and that's fine with both of us. Sometimes now when we are together and silent, I am gripped with panic that it's happened, the thing that other couples warn you about, which is that once the kids are gone, you realize you have nothing to say to each other. But then, like the urge to fight about something unimportant, the feeling passes.

Why didn't my father reply when I asked for the secret of a lasting marriage? Maybe, as with many other things in life, the nonanswer *is* the answer. It is hard to talk about love without bumping into one cliché after another. Perhaps the couple in the De Beers ad are silent because they've run out of ways to say "I love you" without sounding moronic. If you are fortunate, you stay married and life unfolds as the years pass; love is constant, but largely unremarked upon. Remember the 1981 Raymond Carver short-story collection *What We Talk About When We Talk About Love*? My husband and I are nothing like the characters in those stories. Still, I think about that title often. In our particular wonderful, boring, surprising, difficult, enduring relationship, here's what we talk about when we talk about love:

- Who is picking the boys up from the train?
- Do we have enough money to buy a new trampoline?
- Will you zip me up in the back?
- What should we serve your parents for Thanksgiving?

- Do I need to shave?
- Should we invite the new neighbors over for a drink?
- Why is that child so annoying?
- Is tomorrow a recycling day?
- Do you think he needs a throat culture?
- What's her name again?
- Why won't you watch *Game of Thrones* with me?
- Do we have any frozen pineapple?
- Can I wear jeans to this party?
- Will you look at that thing on the dog's paw?
- Where's the checkbook?
- Do we have enough leftovers for dinner?

In other words, all the necessary, quotidian details that make up a partnership—that is love. The reliable, tedious push-and-pull of shared tasks and responsibilities that signal decades of true companionship, inside jokes, and similar views on everything from how to raise a family to whether broccoli is better roasted or steamed. Those are the things we talk about when we talk about love.

Chapter 14

When a Friend Dies Before the Age of Sixty

When a friend dies before the age of sixty, you are wholly unprepared.

You set up a meal train when you learn that he is sick and dozens of people compete to make dinners that they hope will have meaning and leave them in the cooler on the porch between five and six p.m. for the wife and children and visiting relatives to share. You don't know if your friend can eat any of it. You do not ring the doorbell. You include a bottle of wine.

You set up a Facebook group and invite people who

also love your friend to join it so there is one place to get updates and share memories and diverting stories. On the days your friend feels well enough, he reads the posts himself. On the days he doesn't, his wife reads the posts aloud.

You post a funny video of a baby to the group just to make your friend laugh and then wonder if that was a bad idea because maybe babies will remind him of the grandchildren he will never meet.

You just want someone to tell you what to do, knowing that the only thing your friend needs is something you can't give him, which is more time. You try to help in every way you can while suspecting that what you are doing may mean nothing in the grand scheme of things.

You talk to a mutual friend and in the space of forty-five seconds you cry with despair and then gossip about the tragedy-magnet acquaintance who keeps texting for updates even though she barely knows your dying friend. You are grateful that even though the sadness is overwhelming, there is still room for bitchiness, because sometimes bitchiness makes you forget the real stuff.

You want an etiquette book. There is no etiquette book.

You wonder how it is that your friend is dying when

people who are truly horrible get to stay alive. Why is it that this man, who is kind and generous and never stops smiling, who is a coach and a teammate and a husband, brother, father, beloved by all—why is it that he is dying in his fifties and Whitey Bulger got to live so long?

You think about your friend when you meditate and as soon as you wake up and when you are looking at the trees in your backyard and at the way the clouds move across the sky. You think about him lying in the hospital on morphine and the fact that, although he has told his wife that he wants to take every measure possible to prolong his life, maybe he has reached the point when he just wants it to be over.

You are confused when he is released from the hospital after a scary two-week stay that looked like the end. Does this mean he is...all better? You trick your brain into thinking that the illness is behind him. That it was all some sort of cruel test, and he has passed.

You simply have no idea what's best for anyone involved. When your son, who is twenty-one and thinks he is immortal, informs you that he is going skydiving with the son of your dying friend, you are flummoxed. The fact that skydiving by anyone's son is a terrible idea seems beside the point. Surely your friend's son, who is also twenty-one, longs for things that are distracting and life-affirming. You get it. But skydiving! Your husband cautions you about getting involved, being a busybody. But tell that to your imagination. Is a skydiving accident really what your friend's family needs right now? You lobby other mothers behind the scenes to put the kibosh on these plans, not sure if you are doing the right thing.

Your friend's story is no longer his own. His body is no longer his own. You and too many others to count now know about his kidneys and liver and prostate, his heart and lungs, his pain threshold and bowel function. You wonder if he cares that everyone knows these things and at what stage a person is beyond caring.

You think that dying this way—with one dehumanizing test after another as you shuffle off this mortal coil—seems unbearable and wrong. You compose a text to a mutual friend telling her that if you ever get that sick, she should push you in front of a train. But then you delete the text because it seems so insensitive, not to mention false.

You bring another friend up to speed and each time you finish a sentence she replies, "Oh no."

You take a business trip to Texas and have dinner with a college friend who is an oncologist. He listens impassively as you talk about your dying friend. He does not say "Oh no." And he corrects you when you use the word *disease*. "Cancer is not a disease," he says. "Cancer is a process."

You wonder how and when the process will end, and then you feel awful for wondering.

You hear there is a woman at a local nail salon who makes house calls. Would it be weird to send her over to your friend's wife, who rarely leaves his side? Life must go on—isn't that what they say? Does life going on include pedicures?

You marvel at the fact that after the doctors tell your friend there is no longer anything they can do, he simply goes home to wait. While he is waiting, he receives visitors, and he laughs his big regular laugh and gets in and out of the hospital bed and exhibits so many of his normal personality traits that you just know human life is so strange. How can he be so himself and yet so close to not existing altogether?

You try to remember the times in your life when you were waiting for a significant event with an uncertain ETA. Waiting to hear whether you got the job. Waiting to hear if the seller has accepted your offer. Waiting to go into labor. What must it be like, you wonder, to wait for death? You know that you too are waiting for death and that every day your wait is incrementally shortened. But what can it possibly be like to lie there waiting? Do you get one final moment of awareness, and do you recognize it when it comes?

You travel through your days, doing the quotidian things you always do, knowing now that life is both much more beautiful and much more awful than you ever suspected.

You paddle a kayak onto the middle of a lake on a warm August day and you feel guilty, watching your paddle dip in and out of the sparkling water, because you know your friend is lying in a hospital bed in his living room, with a pain pump.

You pour yourself a glass of white wine and it is golden and beautiful in the afternoon light and you feel guilty taking that first sip, because you know your friend cannot do the same.

You walk down a busy street in Manhattan, passing people who are wearing sunglasses and wondering what to have for lunch, traveling in pairs or talking on the phone, smiling and laughing, making plans for the weekend, and you feel guilty.

You think that you are constantly dwelling on the fact that your friend is dying, so imagine how he feels.

You force your own son to listen to updates, even though he doesn't want to think about it, because you believe it's important that he understand. You wonder if that is the right choice, to make him confront this.

He absolutely does not want to discuss it. But when you tell him he needs to go buy a suit that fits properly so he can wear it to the funeral, he does not protest.

You don't ever use the word *death*. No one ever uses the word, at least not while your friend is still alive.

You wonder if a body can ever run out of tears.

You have a business lunch with a new professional acquaintance, and, because you are a fool, you allow the topic of your dying friend to come up. And then you start to cry. This new acquaintance reaches across the table and grasps your arm and says she is so sorry, but you know she's really thinking that you might be deranged.

You read the texts and e-mails and Facebook posts and Caring Bridge messages over and over. There are so many, from people who have loved your friend at every stage of his life, because when you die in your fifties, most of the people who have loved you are still alive. The words are moving and eloquent and you imagine each message is a cupped pair of hands, trying to hold on to your friend as he slips through like water.

You read a description of death in the newspaper, that death is "the last friend." You wonder if that's true.

When your friend dies, on an otherwise ordinary Wednesday evening, you still feel shocked. As if you didn't understand that this was where things were headed all along.

You wake up before dawn one day and remember a poem by Patrick Phillips that you saw on the subway years ago:

Heaven

It will be the past
and we'll live there together.

Not as it was *to live*
but as it is remembered.

It will be the past.
We'll all go back together.

Everyone we ever loved,
and lost, and must remember.

It will be the past.
And it will last forever.

And you hope for your friend, and for yourself, and more than anything else that Patrick Phillips is right.

Chapter 15

What This "Good Enough" Mother Learned from an Extraordinary Babysitter

Over the course of my first two decades as a mother, I employed five babysitters for my three boys. Our first babysitter broke her shoulder in our Brooklyn apartment and threatened to sue us. Our second babysitter was rushed by my husband to the hospital for emergency gallbladder surgery after we came home to find her lying on the floor. Our third babysitter got married, got divorced, got pregnant. Our fourth baby-sitter got pregnant too. Actually, each of our first four babysitters got pregnant while caring for our children. Is that because our chaotic, testosterone-filled house-hold made family life look so . . . appealing? Regardless, it seemed like some kind of weird human-resources record.

Until Renata, that is. Renata didn't get pregnant. Or have emergency surgery or even almost sue us. But she did change the way I think about family and parenting and what being "good enough" really means.

Hiring someone else to take care of your children while you work feels, on good days, like a beautiful act of faith and, on bad days, like every single thing in your life is broken. When Hillary Clinton was running for president and announced that qual-ity, affordable childcare was part of her platform, I thought, *Well, finally!* Any working mother knows that nothing—and I mean nothing—affects her state of mind like the state of her childcare. Why do you think the Obamas had Grandma move into the White House?

When my children were small, I read a magazine article about good-enough parenting. It wasn't so much an article as a gigantic permission slip; I nearly had it tattooed across my forehead. For years, it gave me permission to believe that imperfect and perfect child-rearing were not that far apart. That, absent some spectacular parenting or babysitting failure, my sons would turn out okay.

I'm extremely lucky that I was able to employ a babysitter who came to my house to take care of my kids. It's a luxury many working parents cannot afford. This setup, however, does not eliminate complications, both logistical and emotional. In my experience, a parent's relationship with a caregiver is a constant see-saw between worship and resentment, with gratitude as the fulcrum. In each case, I worshipped my baby-sitter because she did with expert care what I couldn't while I was at work: pour apple juice, supervise cello practice, play Boggle. But I resented her because part of me believed I should have been playing Boggle rather than sitting in a work meeting. Dumb little things like the fact that she left the cello in the car at the end of the day made me quietly enraged, not because I cared where the cello spent the night but because she was not me and I was not there, and the combination of guilt and loss of control made me feel like both the angriest and the pettiest person in the world.

I tried to remind myself that a cello is just a

cello. Good enough is good enough. And I remained detached, with a force field between my heart and my babysitter.

But then came Renata. Over the years, friends would say of their caregivers, "She is just like family!" I'd nod in response, but inside I'd think (a) *Don't lie to me,* and (b) *I must be 75 percent robot.* Because I had never, ever felt that way. But while my heart wasn't paying attention, Renata became just like family. Was it because she once rescued my anxious, sleepless son from a sleepover at two a.m. because I had turned off my phone and he could only reach her? Or because she made me a cake with sliced strawberries on top that spelled out *Happy Birthday, Kristin*? Or because she brought my husband a sandwich every day for a week while he recovered from ACL surgery, knowing it was impossible for him to manage both crutches and lunch?

No. The reason the force field dissolved and gratitude turned to love was that Renata, who arrived when Axel was four and stayed until he was twelve, was so much more than good enough. She was like my sister—funny, kind, interesting, occasionally bossy, consistently reliable, and always, always on our family's side. Which might explain why, before Renata left us, my stoic mother sent me an e-mail that said,

When I think about Renata leaving, I feel like I'm going to cry.

Finally, Renata was a better babysitter than I am a parent. I will always miss her, and miss the way our family felt when she was a part of our daily life. But I will never forget what she taught me: That when it comes to parenting and babysitters and children and love, good enough is good enough. But extraordinary will change your family forever.

Chapter 16

Aging Parents and the Long Goodbye

I. TETHERED

One Christmas when I was in my thirties I descended with my two sisters and our families on our parents' house in Delaware. We all genuinely enjoy one another's company, which is one of the greatest blessings of my adult life. It's not an exaggeration to say that it feels just like a party when we are together, when we allow ourselves to slow down and simply *be*. And while we slow down, time seems like it's speeding up. Because the days we spend together are never long enough.

At least that's how it feels to me. To my mother, apparently, not so much. During this particular "feels just like a party" Christmas, she disappeared for a stretch one afternoon, and I found her stomping around her bedroom, muttering to herself. "What's wrong?" I asked.

She turned to face me. "I always really look forward to when you girls come home," she said quietly. "And then after a while I'm ready for you to leave."

You know those people whose sentimentality is so pronounced, it accompanies them everywhere, like a cloud of perfume that announces their arrival and lingers long after they've left? That is not my mother. Does she bear a very small resemblance to Moira Rose, Catherine O'Hara's character in *Schitt's Creek*? No, I would not say that. She's not at all vain, she's never worn a wig, and she doesn't use words like *heuristic* in everyday conversation. But she does approach life with a determined get-on-with-it-ness. She does not look back; she does not fear change; she does not hold on to things.

She may be disappointed to read that I am fifty-six years old and still not ready for her to leave.

My parents are active, healthy, in their early eighties,

still married, still alive. They live three states away and come to visit for holidays and random weekends, and, pre-coronavirus, my little nuclear family of five would go on vacation with them for a week at least twice a year. Some years, three times. Is this extreme? Shut up. It's not as if we are all living in a motel, in adjoining rooms, like Moira and Johnny Rose and their adult children (although, hello, that could be amazing).

It may be cause or it may be effect but I am tethered to my parents as if we were climbing a mountain together. Naturally, Mom and Dad are in the lead. We all know that one day the rope in front of me will go slack. Who will pull me along then?

A few miles from our house there is a wonderful, weird little cemetery, with gravestones tilting this way and that across a small, uneven clearing of grass, surrounded by woods. It looks completely unplanned, haphazard, as if it spontaneously started growing there one day, like moss on a rock. Some of the grave markers are so small that they remind me of Edith Wharton's pet cemetery at the Mount, her Massachusetts house, where she buried her dogs on a little knoll that she could see from her bedroom window. This is something I am definitely going to do if I ever become as rich as Edith Wharton was; burying a dog in your yard is illegal in my town (I've checked), but if I have enough money, surely I can bribe someone to look the other way.

As I walk through this local cemetery, I get all kinds of ideas. First of all, headstones. This is my very favorite:

THOMAS M. STURGE
Native of England
KILLED
By the falling of a Tree
Oct. 7, 1852
Aged 32 Years

In a modern world where truth has lost its value and we're confronted with conflicting information on just about everything—do fats make you fat? does the separation of powers exist in our country anymore? is Richard Simmons still alive?—I've decided that the inscription on my headstone needs to be like that of Thomas M. Sturge: declarative and specific, leaving no unanswered questions or opportunities for debate. I'm thinking something like this:

KRISTIN van OGTROP
Native of Delaware

DIED SUDDENLY WHILE NAPPING ON THE PORCH
*In the middle of a Wonderful Dream
About Banana Pudding*
April 17, 2064
Age 100 Years (to the day!)

I've also learned from Thomas M. Sturge and his gravesite neighbors that it's possible, with sufficient planning, for whole families to be buried together in what is, for all intents and purposes, a freelance cemetery. Consider the Mead family, who had interesting ideas about first names and were clever enough to be buried together:

Shadrach Mead (lived to be 80)
His wife, Phebe (died at age 87)
Arthur (19 years, 11 months, and 19 days)
Martha (23 years, 6 months)
Harriet (19 years, 9 months, and 15 days)
Josephine (5 years and 9 months)
Willit (1 year, 1 month, and 17 days)

So I have hatched a plan that's even better than living in adjoining rooms in a motel, because it enables me to be tethered to my parents for all of eternity.

I'm going to track down the people who now own my childhood home and ask if they'll let us establish a little van Ogtrop family cemetery at the edge of the backyard, where it would be in the way of no one but the groundhogs who, I'm assuming, still appear every spring. I will write some precise, snappy language for the headstones, which will be no bigger than the ones Edith Wharton designed for her dogs. I don't know why anybody would say no. But if the homeowners or local authorities object, I'm sure we can come up with enough money to bribe them to look the other way.

II. HOUSE WITH LIGHTED WINDOWS

Recently a work acquaintance gave me the following assignment: "Calculate how many times per year you see your mother, then estimate how much longer she might live. You will then have a rough sense of how many more times you will see her during her lifetime."

Why in the world would I ever want to do that?

In our family, there are three unpleasant destabilizers we tend to avoid as much as possible: screaming, shame, and destruction of property. When I was in second grade, one legendary incident involved all of them. It was a weekday, and I wanted to take my yo-yo to school. My father wouldn't let me. As a parent now myself, I will sometimes say no to a request from one of my children without having a good reason; it's like a default *no* that pops out of my mouth before my brain has a chance to actually consider what the kid wants. I inherited this stingy, knee-jerk tendency from my father. Chances are, that morning, Dad didn't have a considered, legitimate reason to forbid me to take the yo-yo to school, and the injustice and capriciousness of his refusal enraged me, just as it enrages my son Axel when I tell him that no, he can't have a snack if he's just brushed his teeth.

Mom was never one to leap to the default *no,* but she stayed out of it as Dad and I both lost our tempers; there was screaming and as I left the house—without my yo-yo—I slammed the storm door so hard that the glass shattered and rained down in a slow-motion, horrifying cascade all over our front steps.

I was absolutely stunned. And then my father became *really* angry, neck-vein-popping angry, angrier at me than he had ever been. We had crossed an uncrossable line. I spent the school day with the heavy knowledge that something unforgivable had happened, and it was all my fault. There would be consequences so severe I couldn't even imagine them.

When I returned home, the shards of glass were

gone, the front steps swept clean, our little house once again snug and neat. The empty frame of the storm door seemed like a weird trick of the eye. Dad, I knew, was at the office. Still, I crossed the threshold with dread. The house was quiet; I found my mother cutting out a skirt pattern on the living-room floor.

"Are you going to kill me?" I said quietly.

She looked up in surprise. "No," she said.

"Is Dad?"

"Of course not." And she smiled and pulled me into her arms.

That was that. I realized for the first time that parents, good parents, help you weather the storm, even if—especially if—you caused it. They keep you on course, the ballast in the hull that prevents unpredictable seas from swamping the boat. Largely unseen, largely unacknowledged, vital to the operation and safety of the crew. Forever.

My mother turned eighty this past spring. Before any of us even had a chance to ask, she announced that she did not want a party. Raised by a strict, domineering father who believed that children should be seen, not heard—and who would rap her knuckles with a butter knife if she didn't keep her left hand in her lap at dinner—Mom started life in the background and remained most comfortable there. She does not need to be in the middle of the action; she is the ballast in the hull. She is steady and calm, polite and proper, although she did recently use the term *shitshow* to describe a flight on American Airlines, which proves that, even if you've known someone for fifty-six years, she can still surprise you.

She raised three hardheaded, feminist daughters and has never questioned our capabilities. The subtext of most of our conversations is this:

You are amazing.
You can handle that.
You will figure it out.
You will succeed.

Recently I texted my mother and two sisters to say that the weight I had been for nearly my whole life, from the age of eighteen on, was a thing of the past; my body had decided to be five pounds heavier, and those five pounds had come to rest in a squishy lump on my lower back. If I look at my backside in the mirror and foolishly shake my hips, this squishy lump jiggles at me. Which might be amusing under different circumstances. Like if it were happening to someone else. After they read the text, my sisters, who are younger than I am and have not yet developed squishy lumps, did the considerate thing and voiced their sympathy. Then our mother chimed in: *Best to just adjust your expectations and enjoy life. I think you all look great.*

Her three daughters each have little bits of her: Claire has her strong legs and Valerie has her nice fingernails and I have her pinkie toe that looks like the protuberance growing from the eye of a potato that has been in the pantry for too long. But those are just physical things. We also have everything she taught us, such as how to do the following:

- diaper a baby
- shorten a hem
- run a family
- set a table
- write a condolence note
- make cocktail conversation
- iron a shirt
- arrange flowers
- bake a ham
- act rationally in the face of chaos
- be assertive
- comfort a crying child
- eat healthily
- value honesty
- be frank

- feed the birds
- make curtains for a nursery
- host Thanksgiving
- think out of the box
- swaddle a newborn
- find delight in little things
- act silly
- communicate clearly
- multitask
- tackle a big project
- relax, if and when the occasion calls for it

She showed me how to be a wife and a mother and a woman in the world. She did it all first, and in almost all things, except for drinking skim milk, which is disgusting, I try to follow the example she has set.

It is truly unbelievable to me that there will come a time when I cannot pick up the phone, call my mother, and ask whether that leggy, invasive flower she gave me for my perennial garden is called lychnia or lychnis. I can never remember, but she always does.

There are indignities, physical and emotional, that have befallen me during this time of life, and when they appear I say to myself, *Well, Mom never had to deal with any of this, or she would have prepared me.* However, when I ask her about flaky skin on my shins or night sweats or unexplained bouts of rage, she will nod and say, "Oh, yes, that happened to me too."

Which leads me to wonder what else I don't know about my mother.

Some nights when I head home from the train at the end of a workday, I stop on the sidewalk to stare into the lighted windows of my favorite house, a shingled Victorian with a steep roof and intricate leaded windows set far back from the street on a flat lot dotted with majestic old trees. I wonder what it must be like to live there. In my imagination, life there is rich, and orderly, and wonderful. But I don't know who owns this house and so must content myself with the view from the sidewalk. That is how I feel about Mom: She is a house with lighted windows. Although I can admire things from a distance, I will never understand what it's like to live inside.

III. LAUGHTER AND FORGETTING

Last winter I went skiing with my father, and as we waited at the bottom of the lift we couldn't help but notice the little girl a dozen yards away who was having a terrible morning. Putting on ski equipment is bad enough if you are an adult who understands the relationship between effort and reward and knows not to throw tantrums in public. But if you are four years old and clearly tired, it's a whole different story. As anyone within earshot could tell. There was no mollifying this child. Her exasperated mother seemed to have given up, so naturally my father felt it was his duty to get involved. What Dad considers a "helpful person," others might call an "aggressive weirdo," which means that, occasionally, he can be admirable and infuriating at the same time.

In his heavy ski boots Dad clomped over to the girl, reached into his jacket, and produced a Starlight peppermint. He handed it to her and smiled. She glared back. He smiled wider. She frowned. It was fascinating to watch—like a game of chicken between amateur dictators. With quick fingers, never breaking her gaze, the girl unwrapped the mint and popped it in her mouth. Then she smiled.

Dad clomped back over to me, triumphant. "Let's go!" he said. And we got onto the ski lift and zoomed away.

The little girl's mother was busy with another child and missed the whole episode. Was her daughter allergic to mint, or prone to choking, or forbidden to eat candy? Who knows! Because of course my father didn't ask. The older he gets, the more I'm convinced that somewhere in the deep recesses of his brain there is a section called I Don't Give a Shit. It's right next to Slight Cognitive Decline. Taken together, these parts of his brain may explain what happened in Aruba on his seventieth birthday.

Although my father was born and raised on that tiny island off the coast of Venezuela, all he ever wanted was to be American, and when he came to the United States for college and met my mother, he was so embarrassed by his origins on a windy little disk of sand overrun by goats that he lied and told her he was from California. Eventually the truth came out, as it always does. As a high-school cheerleader turned home-ec major from Delaware, my mother thought Aruba, as a birthplace and an idea, sounded exotic, amazing, and maybe even a little dangerous, which was confirmed the first time she visited the island and was bitten by a scorpion, right on her breast.

After he married my mother and became American-ish, Dad seemed happy to keep Aruba in the past. But when he turned seventy, my sisters and I cooked up a meaningful, memorable splurge: we took everybody—husbands, children, and Grammy and Opie, as their grandchildren call them—to the island to celebrate. The Aruba we visited clearly was not my father's Aruba. Now the goats are outnumbered by tourists who fill the giant beachfront high-rises and nonde-script condominium complexes, which is where we found ourselves staying for the week.

A few days into the vacation, my father got up early to go to the gym. As I was preparing breakfast in the little condo kitchen, I heard my son Hugo say, "What's Opie doing over there?"

I looked out the window to the identical building across the way, and it took me a moment to process what I saw: my father, sitting alone at the breakfast table, in someone else's condo.

I called to my mother. She joined me at the window. I gestured. "Mom? What's he doing?"

Dad crossed his legs, turned the page of the newspaper, took a sip of orange juice from a glass on the table.

"I have no idea," Mom said.

This is a man who lives in a state of constant preparedness. Visit his house and you'll find that he's constructed an elaborate framework of how-tos and reminders, a bulwark against cognitive decline. There are Post-It notes everywhere: by the light switches and thermostat and back door. With instructions written in ALL CAPS, all the time.

As his daughter, I will stick a Post-It on my dishwasher that says CLEAN or masking tape with GORGONZOLA SAUCE FOR STEAK written in Sharpie on an otherwise mysterious Pyrex container in the freezer. I don't have tennis balls hanging from the ceiling of my garage to tell me exactly where to park, as my father does, but then I suppose he has not written down outfit combinations so he can remember from one week to the next the things he should wear that don't make him feel misshapen, misguided, or two hundred years old. Do I do that? I'm not telling.

We are preparing, all of us, for the time brain function takes its leave, and that preparation feels like a very, very long goodbye.

When my father realized his mistake that morning in Aruba (identical buildings; door left open by trusting fellow vacationers who happened to have orange juice in the refrigerator), he laughed and laughed and laughed. That is one of his best qualities: his ability to laugh even harder than the rest of us when we are laughing entirely at his expense.

But as I watched my father's good-natured reaction to his mistake, a very small voice in my head whispered, *All right, then. Here it comes.*

My paternal grandmother was a little firecracker who attended all of her sons' baseball games wearing pretty cotton dresses belted around her teeny-tiny waist, sitting all alone in the bleachers because her family was too embarrassed to be seen with her when she hollered insults at the inferior players. She developed Alzheimer's in her late seventies and, in her final years, stopped speaking English altogether. She would sit in the corner at family parties, muttering in Dutch, counting her seven children on seven bony fingers, saying their names in birth order. When she got through all seven, she immediately started again.

My maternal grandmother had early-onset Alzheimer's disease and died in her sixties, when I was eight. I have very few memories of her; to me she was a silent creature in a wheelchair, her four-foot-eleven frame hunched nearly into a ball. But I've heard enough stories to know that she had been a vibrant woman who loved gardening and racing sailboats. When I was born, she told my mother that she couldn't wait until I was old enough to go downtown with her and have lunch at the department store, just the two of us. I would wear white gloves, she said.

When we got married I blithely announced to my husband that, since both of my grandmothers had Alzheimer's, he should prepare himself to change my diaper one day. At the time I thought it was funny, as most things having to do with aging are funny when you are in your twenties and mortality is a concept reserved for the kind of philosophy seminar you didn't take in college because it seemed too hard, not to mention boring. Now, in my fifties, I consider the tightening grip of Alzheimer's disease and know that very little, if anything, is funny about it. But until the official diagnosis comes, I plan to laugh as much as I can.

IV. PARENTS AND YOUR PREFRONTAL CORTEX

The instant your children become teenagers, all anybody talks about is the prefrontal cortex. Few people actually know where it is or how it functions, but everyone understands that each dumb thing a teenager does—in fact, each dumb thing any human being does before turning twenty-six—can be traced back to a prefrontal cortex that is not yet fully developed. It is during this unformed time of life that a young person believes her parents are complete morons who know exactly nothing. They don't get it! She stares out the window of her bedroom—well, she does if she is Kristin van Ogtrop— as dusk drapes the world in melancholy, listening to music that evokes a longing in her that her parents couldn't possibly understand. Her whole life is going to be like a Joni Mitchell song—no, wait, a Janis Ian song, with all its loneliness, heartbreak, and drama—and there is no way in the world her parents could possibly know that, as she does with a terrible teenage certainty.

But remember the words of Mark Twain: "When I was a boy of fourteen, my father was so ignorant I could hardly stand to have the old man around. But when I got to be twenty-one, I was astonished at how much the old man had learned in seven years." By the time a person is twenty-six and her prefrontal cortex has finished its development, almost overnight her parents become right about much of life. Suddenly she is mature and wise enough to apologize for past mistakes, like the time she had a party when they were out of town and Alex Calvert and his drunk friends wrote profane messages all over her mother's birthday calendar. She goes off to college and hears hair-raising stories about the mothers and fathers of some of her new acquaintances and thinks, *Oh my God, there are so many screwed-up families in the world! Thank heavens mine isn't one of them.*

But then she matures a little more, and the shades begin to slip from her eyes. With a fully formed prefrontal cortex and the inchoate wisdom of young adulthood, she sees that her parents are neither always wrong nor always right but simply terrific, flawed human beings. She is different from them, and there are aspects of her lifestyle and belief system that they fail to appreciate, which can feel like a betrayal. And that is true even if everybody gets along and takes big "feels just like a party" family trips to Aruba.

Then more years pass and eventually similarities and differences cease to matter, because the people who make it to middle age with loving parents who are still alive are the lucky ones. Gratitude takes over: gratitude for the people who gave you life and sacrificed so much for your health and happiness; gratitude that you remain on speaking terms.

It is truly unbelievable that my parents will one day die and I will never see them again on this earth. As I write this, my husband and I—in our mid-fifties—both have two living parents. Everyone is still here! I've never looked it up, but I suspect that makes us statistical anomalies. And it has established in us, over time, a false sense that if our parents haven't left yet, they never will.

V. THE LONG GOODBYE

My father's entire family is very big on speeches. Whenever we get together for Boxing Day—my father and his six siblings, plus spouses, children, and grandchildren—someone is always tapping a knife against a glass and then standing up and talking in a sentimental fashion for five minutes. And then Uncle Chuck, who is not Dutch but is our most enthusiastic family member, will break into "Lang Zal Ze Leven in de Gloria"—which as far as I know is how you sing "Happy Birthday" in Holland; go figure—and we all sing along.

To celebrate my father's eightieth birthday, sixteen of us had dinner at an inn in my parents' town. I was sitting next to Dad in the middle of the table and noticed some folded yellow legal paper peeking from his breast pocket. After dessert, he tapped his knife against his glass, smoothed out the paper, and began to read. It was the story of his life, divided into three phases: Aruba, young adulthood, maturity. He spoke of hard work and perseverance and gratitude and, most of all, love.

Eyes never leaving the page, he read, "'As I continue to age, I revel in the successes of my children and grandchildren and that makes my journey all worthwhile, and when I go to the big house in the sky at the end of my journey, I can be proud that the journey was worthwhile and complete.'"

When he finished reading, he thanked us for listening; I glanced over and spied this at the bottom of the page: *2/24/1939–?*

That. That is the part that makes me cry.

At the end of the table sat my youngest son, Axel, and my sister Claire's two boys, rambunctious kids who have been known to act like juvenile delinquents when they are together. But they had sat silently, listening to their grandfather. Afterward, Axel left his seat and crawled into my lap. "That was so sad," he said. "I don't want Opie to go away."

I didn't tell my son that, if Opie is allowed the opportunity, he will say a final goodbye that will be much more elaborate than that, maybe accompanied by trumpets or a mariachi band. On his eightieth birthday Opie was just practicing for what he'll do when he turns ninety, and the speech he reads then will be twice as long. Followed by a magic act, or Cirque du Soleil.

My mother, who has a limited tolerance for people who give toasts, does not approve of the elaborate goodbye; when she thinks my father is taking too long to leave a party, she will go out and sit in the car, hoping this will move Dad along. She can be very sneaky. When I turned forty she made a scrapbook for me, which at first seemed like a very thoughtful gesture. It obviously took months of effort; she'd hunted down every elementary-school report card and swim-meet ribbon and letter home from college she could find among the decades of accumulated memorabilia and crap that my existence had brought into her life. It was an amazing gift, really, and I was deeply touched.

Still, I had the nagging sense that it meant she was . . . finished with me. After I unwrapped it, I gave her my most piercing stare. "Are you putting me up for adoption?" I asked.

She rolled her eyes and laughed, and I laughed too.

But I'm not sure she ever answered.

VI. THE URGENT VERSUS THE IMPORTANT

When my father reflects on death, his arrival at the big house in the sky, he frequently mentions how much he is looking forward to reuniting with his parents. They died thirty years ago! Has he been longing for them all this time? My neighbor Nancy is about the same age as my parents and I once remarked to her that it seemed crazy to be in my fifties and still need my parents. She replied, "When you're in your seventies you still need your parents."

What happens when you need your parents and they are no longer there? Do memories fill the gap? Who is there to reassure, to comfort and guide you, to say, "Oh yes, that happened to me too"?

My parents are currently preparing to move into one of those places where a bunch of old people live together in what is essentially a giant dormitory where they can take classes and play contract bridge and attend choral concerts in the auditorium off the lobby, right next to the gift shop. I am never sure what to call a place like that. Assisted living? Adult-care facility? Retirement home? None of these terms seems entirely accurate. Let's just call it the Inevitable. I toured the Inevitable with my mother and the place looked nice enough; there is a sunny art studio for Mom and, for Dad, limitless possibilities for aggressive helpfulness—holding the elevator for slow-moving residents, picking up fallen canes, pushing stubborn wheelchairs for people too tired to object.

Mom and Dad don't talk much about dying, but when they do, it's all business, the way they talk about moving into the Inevitable: it's a necessary step, if one they don't particularly want to take. They are people of strong religious faith, which I know helps. Sometimes my dad jokes about death; this is comforting, but weird—since death might be the ultimate not-laughing matter—and it makes me wonder whether every joke he has ever told has had an undercurrent of sadness, which then leads me to question too many things about my past and entire existence, so best not to think about that.

If you have had a happy childhood, there is a decent chance you will grow up to replicate fundamental aspects of your parents' lives; many of their choices look appealing and you turned out more or less okay. You follow their lead, but at a distance; you don't live in a Schitt's Creek motel with them like the Rose family but a few states or maybe even a continent away, with children and storm doors and birthday calendars all your own. You have less time to devote to them, the people who showed you how to do all that in the first place. It seems like such a flawed system. And yet we repeat it, generation after generation.

I am lucky to have living parents, and it is too easy to forget that. An insightful friend once told me that we all fall prey to the bad habit of letting the urgent override the important. That stopped me in my tracks; letting the urgent override the important could be my theme song. One day, no doubt, I will look back on my life and wonder whether that bad habit colored many of my relationships, including—or most of all— the one I had with my parents.

But prioritizing the urgent over the important is self-protection. You know what's coming for your mother and your father, and, oh yes, it's coming for you too. You are powerless against the forward momentum. And powerlessness is the most awful feeling in the world. The urgent things that take up our days—return that phone call, clean that bathroom, roast that cauliflower

Chapter 17

Dear Searching: Advice for a Midlife Career Crisis

Q: I have had a long, productive, happy career working for a large corporation. I used to think my job was perfect and that it would last forever. Now, for reasons I'd rather not get into, I find myself unemployed. But I'm not ready to retire. How do I know what to do next?

Sincerely,

Searching in San Francisco

Kristin van Ogtrop

Dear Searching in San Francisco,

Sweetheart, have you come to the right place! I understand your predicament. It is so confusing when you realize that, like healthy teeth and your child's blind regard for you, the perfect job is not destined to last forever. Sadly, the world of our youth, where a person could graduate from the University of Delaware with an engineering degree, work for DuPont until the age of sixty-five, then retire with a putter in one hand and a highball glass full of whiskey in the other—well, that world just doesn't exist anymore. Or maybe that was just my youth and my own grandfather. Never mind! There is something both liberating and terrifying about being unemployed in middle age, when you know just enough about the working world and what you need from it to be dangerous to yourself and others. That is to say, it's entirely possible that you've come to believe, in your hard-earned, midlife wisdom, that whatever you do next—as retirement looms closer by the hour— must provide your days with *meaning*. (Maybe free yoga classes too. But definitely meaning.) Meaning! What is meaning, anyway? Do you recognize it when you've found it?

Searching in San Francisco, I'm sure you are wrestling with these same issues in this uncertain time.

276

I must confess that even I—your esteemed advice columnist who can't do yoga because of a torn labrum in her shoulder that her family doubts is real—fell victim to the belief that the way one spends one's daylight hours should have meaning and that somewhere out there, just waiting for me, was the job that would provide it. For many years, I too worked for a large corporation, and there I reached a point when my employer was happy to pay me to go away and never come back. (See chapter 6.) I set out on a quest to find my One True Thing, keeping in mind these cautionary words of Yogi Berra: "You've got to be very careful if you don't know where you are going, because you might not get there."

My youngest son, Axel, is a kind, charming child who will sometimes say, with great authority, things that turn out not to be true. For instance, he once told me that the Mandarin word *si* has three different meanings: "death," "table," and "four." These three things seem totally random and unrelated, and a quick Google search revealed that, sadly, Axel was once again exchanging fabrication for fact. For a while, his gullible mother believed him, though perhaps that was because this linguistic improbability provided an apt metaphor for how I felt about myself as I was ending my magazine career. I very much hoped that, depending on the context, *Kristin* could be "nonprofit executive," "stay-at-home mom," and "generously compensated head of communications for a gigantic company that was flush with cash but also 'good.'" Simply change the setting and expectations, and *Kristin* could mean any of those things. Turns out *si* doesn't mean three random, unrelated things, and *Kristin* doesn't either.

Searching in SF, right now your options may seem varied and abundant, which is both exciting and scary. Is it possible you have peaked, that your best days are behind you? Maybe. But let's not dwell on that! Instead, I encourage you to follow my eight-step plan to finding meaning in the days ahead. (Bonus: If you're like me, along the way you will also learn to sleep peacefully at night because you didn't waste the previous sixteen hours doing something soul-crushing while surrounded by morons. Honestly, you are already in a much better place.)

(1) Remember the Person You Once Were

This first step—in which you set aside all practicalities and take a long look at your soul—can be accompanied by euphoria and optimism. (See "pay me to go away and never come back," above.) You may have a list of worries—that your days will lack discipline; that you will feel lonely; that 80 percent of your wardrobe is dressy, corporate-lady clothes, so what are you supposed to wear to elementary-school pickup? That you will eventually go broke. But, for now, the time before you seems limitless, and that is positively intoxicating. As you contemplate the future, it's helpful to look into your past in order to understand who you were before you became corrupted by Microsoft Outlook and a fondness for expensive shoes.

I'm not necessarily recommending that you repeat my journey, Searching in San Francisco, but once upon a time I was an earnest graduate student living in a dark apartment in a scary neighborhood, eating meatless meals and reading poems that weren't pretty or accessible so I could pretend to understand them. I was twenty-six years old and really wanted to become an intellectual. This was, of course, before I gained the self-awareness to realize that I am not an intellectual, just a smartish person who likes to read. And believe me, there is a giant difference.

But as I was leaving my job I wondered: Is it too late to go back to that life? Not to quasi-vegetarianism or dark apartments, but to the life of the mind. When does the window of neuroplasticity slam shut, and was there still time to pry it open? Shortly after I decided to quit, I went to a talent show at a summer camp and listened to a man sing a Schubert song, in German, about a guy who falls in love with a maiden who doesn't love him back, so he drowns himself in a brook. What the singer lacked in natural talent, he made up for in earnest intention. Just like me in graduate school. I was mesmerized. In a flash, it came to me: *I'm going to learn German and sing tragic Schubert songs too!* The following afternoon I stumbled upon my son Owen, who was a college senior, reading Emily Dickinson. I realized the only Emily Dickinson poem I could remember was the one with the fly in it that any dummy who took high-school English could recite. I said to myself: *I will devote entire afternoons to reading Emily Dickinson! And not just the three poems everyone has heard of! I will try once again to live the life of the mind and become a true intellectual.*

Schubert in the original German is still on my to-do list. As for Dickinson, I made my best attempt. But I got only as far as the poem that begins "I'm Nobody! Who are you?" when somewhere deep inside me a chord was struck, and I felt too sorry for myself to continue.

(2) Take a Moment to Just Be in the Present

My dear Searching in San Francisco, up to this point, your life has probably been governed by unrealistic deadlines, farcical "urgent" e-mails from the CEO's office, and meetings scheduled for the week after next where you will have to tell some hateful person from the finance office how you are going to cut six hundred thousand dollars from the budget. Or maybe that's me again? Anyway, chances are you have not spent a lot of time enjoying the Present, that magical place where some people manage to live and where you supposedly can focus on nothing but breathing in and out and staying in your pajamas until noon. As soon as I left my job, I got a text from my friend Dan, who had retired early after a dissatisfying career in order to live in the Present. *Great news, congratulations!* his text read. *Being and doing might be best, but just being is pretty great, too.*

No doubt you have other things to do besides lounge around in your pj's breathing in and out. Eating, for instance. I have always liked to cook and after I quit my job I realized that *being,* for me, involved a lot of time thinking about food. I planned elaborate meals that felt thrilling and naughty to make in the middle of the week, and when I went to the grocery store to get my ingredients—for just one dinner, not a whole week's worth of food written out in a long list, organized by sections—I strolled the aisles in search of what I needed, wandering happily, no longer the time-pressed harridan who zoomed through the store like a heat-seeking missile. Occasionally I arrived at the grocery store with no dinner plans whatsoever, knowing inspiration would eventually strike. For example, one day as I contemplated the fish-counter offerings at my local market, I remembered the cod with jalapeño butter my friend Chrissie had made years ago. I texted Chrissie, then scrolled through my photos in case I had a picture of the recipe. While I waited to hear back from Chrissie I wandered into the vast olive oil section and read a few labels. Did you know, Searching in San Francisco, that there are about thirty thousand varieties of olive oil? I recalled my mother telling me that *60 Minutes* said we shouldn't be getting olive oil from Italy anymore because of the Mafia or something. I tried to call Mom to find out what sort of olive oil I should buy instead, but she didn't pick up, so I stood right there in the aisle and looked that up on my phone too.

You'll see: when you live in the Present, you have all the time in the world.

Like cooking, other domestic tasks can flip from drudgery to delight if done in the middle of the day on a Wednesday instead of at nine o'clock on Sunday night while you're also planning the family's dinners for the week and yelling at your kids to get in bed. I'm talking about ironing, of course. As I maneuvered my hot iron across cotton shirts and linen napkins, I felt the calm of easily achievable results that were completely within my control. It was relaxing to be ironing and cooking, two tasks I am fairly good at, without a management consultant telling me that the way I was doing things—in fact, the way I had done things for all of my adult life—was much too slow and definitely too expensive. Apologies, Searching in SF, if you have spent your career working as a management consultant, because I'm sure you're a wonderful person. But boy, do I have stories.

Not everything came as easily to me as ironing and cooking. One week I tried re-caulking the tile around my kitchen sink, which I had never done before. That was a disaster.

(3) Check Off an Item on Your Bucket List. Try Something Fun!

Have you always wanted to take tai chi? Learn how to knit? Become a master gardener? Now's the time!

When people asked me as I was leaving my job what I planned to do next, I would answer, "Take a pottery class!" This was a great way to ensure that the other person would look confused or appalled and abruptly change the subject. But I meant it. As soon as I escaped the bowels of corporate hell, I enrolled in a pottery class that met at my local art center every Tuesday morning from nine till noon.

The studio was big and sunny with old metal stools and long, high tables and the wonderful, chalky smell of an elementary-school art room. The six other students in the class had been studying with Susan, our Hungarian instructor, for years. From my first day, I was the bull in the china shop, loudly calling for help to cut the clay or find the right glaze. The others worked with quiet purpose, side-eyeing me with curiosity, wondering when the moment might come that I'd stumble into the giant shelving unit that held their creations ready for firing and bring weeks of work crashing down. Susan was patient, warm, and welcoming while constantly suggesting that my creations could use a little *oomph*. "That's nice," she would say carefully, "but I think you could add more texture."

Three semesters in Susan's class was all I needed to discover that I simply could not make the image in my head match what came out of my hands. Which was a fairly apt metaphor for that particular stage of my life. But don't be discouraged, dear Searching in San Francisco! I'm sure this will not happen to you.

(4) Talk to Lots of People

Let's revisit that meaning you're now determinedly seeking. Surely there is a job out there, one for which you are supremely well qualified, that will provide it. Still, after you leave the career that dominated your adult life and begin to figure out what comes next, you worry that you will miss the mark. What if you plug your list of talents and interests into a career version of Waze and still end up in the wrong place? Destiny Boulevard in Wakefield, let's say, when you are meant to go to Destiny Avenue in Wakeland? That's where your friends come in. As you're settling—or is it sinking?—into this next phase of your life, you may find that not only is Waze taking you to the wrong destination, but the road itself is foggy, winding, and marked by potholes so deep that you could break an axle or, even worse, fall in and never be seen again. It can be helpful during this uncertain time, just as in many other times of life, to turn to your friends for guidance.

The danger of spending most of your adult life in one career where your success seems predetermined is that you begin to forget about humility. About failure. You don't realize it, but you develop the belief that if you can succeed at X, then surely you can succeed at Y, even if X and Y bear little resemblance to each other. My husband tells me this is true of lots of rich men who buy sports teams, especially the teams he roots for. Bidding farewell to your longtime career is an excellent way to squelch that type of thinking. Perhaps you have not left your job in order to seek out humility, but if you wait long enough, humility will find you.

As my severance package dwindled, I reached a point where I began to wonder whether I was good at anything at all besides being a magazine editor, the job I'd held for twenty-five years. Was I the only woman on the planet with a skill set so narrow that I was capable of excelling at precisely one thing? I polled my friends, asking them to list the skills they had that had nothing to do with their current professional lives. Here are a few of the responses I got back:

Jenny
- applying moisturizer twice daily
- getting babies to sleep
- making sentimental toasts

Courtney
- finding the right, thoughtful gifts for a person
- spotting terrific old chairs
- learning Romance languages

Missy
- cooking for large crowds
- packing groceries

- writing thank you notes, heartfelt letters, and eulogies
  (*Little-known fact,* Missy added, *I also know how to use the paint mixer at Home Depot.*)

Searching in San Francisco, I would highly recommend this exercise. With respect to figuring out your future, it might lead you nowhere, but on some of your darker days, you can remind yourself that yes, there are things you are good at—just look at your list. Here's mine:

- cutting wrapping paper in a straight line
- spelling weird last names that have too many consonants and not enough vowels
- remembering if a couple is still married
- crimping pie crust
- curling my eyelashes without flinching
- recycling

(5) Volunteer!

While you are struggling to figure out who you are and what you're actually good at, it can be helpful to hit Pause and take a look around you. After all, Searching, although you may be sad and lost in a way that feels unbecoming for a middle-aged, self-actualized woman, you don't have to go far to find others who need help more than you do.

A few months after I quit working, a Syrian refugee family moved to my little town. I joined the volunteers who had banded together to assist them, and my job was helping with groceries. Every Wednesday at ten a.m., I would pull up to the house where they had settled and pick up the husband, the wife, and their two-year-old daughter and take them shopping. They spoke no English and I spoke no Arabic, though we smiled at each other a lot. Well, everyone smiled except for the daughter, a beautiful little girl with big eyes and soft curly hair who would stare at me from her car seat in the back with an expression that said, *Your charms don't work on me, lady.* Sometimes we drove to a local grocery store and sometimes we went to a halal market, where the husband would speak in rapid Arabic with the owner and I would wander the aisles, looking at the bins of pistachios and dried dates and spices whose names I couldn't make out.

What did I learn? I learned that if you are standing in the medicine aisle at Costco and, despite your best pantomime, you simply cannot understand what your Arabic-speaking companion is trying to tell you, he can type the Arabic word for "sinus" into Google Translate and you'll discover, with delight, that the English phrase that pops up on your phone is "pockets of nose." I learned to love halloumi and how to say "No problem" in Arabic. I learned that I know nothing about Syria, that it's possible to feel embarrassed just because you are American, and that, even after vacuuming, my car still looks so dirty as to be disturbing to people who don't know me well. But most of all, I learned that when the man sitting beside you in the front seat of your dirty car has been tortured before fleeing his home country, it puts your own search for *direction* and *meaning* into perspective.

And so there is guilt.

Besides feeling guilty about being a privileged American and having a filthy car, I also felt guilty about my dogs. Has your heart ever been broken, Searching, by a situation that you brought on yourself? It was four months after I quit my job that our puppy slipped beneath the ice of a frozen lake and drowned (see chapter 11). I was not only heartbroken but filled with a long list of if-onlys that I could not sweep from my mind. I decided that the best way to make things right, karmically, was to volunteer for Guiding Eyes for the Blind, where our dog had begun his short life. And so every Monday I drove to the Guiding Eyes training facility and assisted the full-time team in the kennels. The work was methodical, with results that were visible and immediate. It was like ironing a linen napkin, but with barking.

One morning as I drove to the kennels, I heard an interview on NPR with Bono and the Edge from U2. Suddenly I remembered that I had met Bono back in my magazine days when my company hosted a dinner for him with a handful of editors. In my car, wearing smelly jeans and waterproof boots, I recalled sitting in an expensive Manhattan restaurant at a big square table with one of the most famous musicians in the world directly across from me. I didn't know what was more amazing: how much my life had changed, or how little my previous life mattered. When I arrived at the kennel and pulled the volunteer smock on over my clothes, I was just another dog lover—one with a wounded heart and time on her hands—and my past had become completely irrelevant.

(6) Try a Vision Quest for Mental Clarity

By now you might be wondering: *What the hell with all these steps? Is it really this complicated? Should I just get over my fear of aloneness and hunger and sign up for a vision quest?*
Yes!
Maybe you are the kind of person, Searching in

San Francisco, who knows all about vision quests. Mine was a quickie, one-day affair, essentially a drive-through for cheaters who are afraid of fasting. As in, it is indeed possible that I filled a big insulated thermos with coffee and milk to drink in the car on the way to the park where I hoped to find clarity in the unfamiliar woods on that June day despite having been instructed to fast by our leader, the wise and wonderful Chiara.

It was from Chiara I learned that when you embark on a vision quest, the most important thing is to maintain a willingness to believe that anything might be possible, not unlike your state of mind when you quit your job because you thought the Mandarin word *si* could mean multiple things. To start the day we all sat in a circle and Chiara—tall and gentle, part crossing guard, part hospital chaplain—talked about the four cardinal directions and what they meant. I was focusing hard on not feeling hungry and wondering why Chiara neglected to mention bears, rapists, or poisonous snakes, so I caught only bits of what she was saying. North seemed to signify adulthood, west was death and rebirth, south was childhood and sensuality, and east—well, I was thinking about eggs Benedict and that one went in one ear and out the other. Chiara asked which direction we would head in so she could mark it on a map. "Be back at two thirty," she instructed. "If you are more than five minutes late, we come looking for you."

There was one other thing Chiara said: "Everything that wants to be seen by you wants to be seen for a reason, and you need to greet the things you see." Which meant that when I saw the bobcat blocking my path, instead of feeling frightened or tempted to blow the plastic whistle that hung around my neck, I said, "Hello, bobcat. I thought you were a lion but now I realize there are no lions in Putnam County. Thank you for showing up today. You've made fasting totally worth it."

He didn't answer but merely padded away, probably because he suspected my sincerity on that final point.

After I saw the bobcat, my vision quest became a bit less dramatic. I sat on a giant, flat rock where I wrote in my journal and listened to a mourning dove call and watched dragonflies zigzag in the air above me. I found some owl pellets that I pulled apart; they contained teeny-tiny bones that filled me with awe until I realized I didn't have any Purell. I thought about my family and my career and my uncertain future, but mostly I thought about whether I should fast more often, just for kicks. When it was nearly two thirty, I found this weird, pouch-like nest hanging from a spindly young birch and saw that it contained five perfect, speckled eggs. I decided on the spot that the eggs represented the five members of my family and that I should turn around. Honestly, you can turn anything into a sign if you try hard enough. It just takes imagination.

At the end of the day, Chiara gave us one final instruction. "Ask yourself," she said, "who came into the woods today? Who left? And what's next?" And then she gave me a hug and a meaningful look, as if I already knew the answers.

(7) If You Have Pets and Children, Find Out Whether They Are Truly the Creatures You Want to Spend All Your Waking Hours With

Do you have children, Searching? Pets? Maybe you are a sharp-edged, unfettered woman who limits herself to houseplants so you can leave town at a moment's notice when the college friend who made it big invites you to Turks and Caicos. No one to clutter your world, talk back, steal your phone charger, or leave the gas tank empty. No dependent who needs to be fed several times a day or rushed to the emergency animal hospital in Connecticut because it's nine p.m. and the grape that rolled off the kitchen counter was gobbled up by a Labrador retriever who will eat anything, even things that may—or may not! but why gamble?—do serious damage to his kidneys.

Grape-eating notwithstanding, most dogs are plenty smart. But, after months of study, I began to question whether a dog is a proper replacement for a coworker. I'm not sure a dog, even a very smart dog, will pull his weight. After I quit my job, my most constant companions were my son Axel, who was nine, and my dog Iggy, who was—like me—enjoying a healthy middle age. Meaning Iggy was wise, intuitive, and no longer inclined to do anything he didn't want to do. Axel spent most of the day in school, so Iggy and I had a lot of alone time. In fact, I had so much alone time with Iggy, I grew to believe that, at any moment, he was about to speak. And I don't mean *speak* as in "bark." I mean I thought he was about to say something, out loud, using his canine mouth to form human words. Why did I believe this? Because, absent human coworkers, I talked to Iggy all day long. And in response, he would gaze at me soulfully, never breaking eye contact, with an expression that said, *I know exactly what you mean.* As the months dragged on, every day we drew one day closer to Iggy being able to speak and to Kristin losing her marbles.

Unlike Iggy, Axel could be parsimonious with his emotional support. When I told my youngest son that I had quit my job, I felt like the character of Buddy in the movie *Elf*. After Buddy spends his first night with his biological father, he composes, on the Etch A Sketch, an exciting list of activities for them to do together. Like Buddy, I naively assumed that my family would be thrilled—*thrilled*—to spend more time with me. And, like Buddy, I was underwhelmed by the reaction I received. When I delivered the news, the first words that popped out of Axel's mouth were "What if you can't get another job?"

Perhaps a child is not a replacement for coworkers either. I'm sure you believe, as I do, that the ideal coworker does not catastrophize in such a way or whine or demand that you make his lunch every day because the school food is cold and tastes like plastic. The ideal coworker does not request ridiculously expensive Adidas Ultraboost sneakers just because some of his friends have them or negotiate for more screen time by promising to finish reading the Hunger Games series.

And the ideal coworker is fun.

It's not that I imagined I would greet Axel every day after school wearing a clown costume and holding a plate of warm gingersnaps. But I tried to make life interesting. I would walk down to the elementary school to pick him up, and sometimes instead of heading straight home we would go on a little surprise adventure (buying Halloween pumpkins! going out for ice cream!) that Axel would pretend to enjoy. I quickly realized that my role was not Provider of Fun but Provider of Structure. And I love structure. However, filling my days with a boy and a dog, following a structure built around their needs, just didn't feel like enough. I knew what I was doing was important. But that's not the same as enough.

Then came the solar eclipse. It was August 21, 2017, a Monday, which meant I spent the morning at Guiding Eyes for the Blind. As always, I listened to the radio while I drove to the kennels and heard that people all over the country had worked themselves into a lather trying to buy last-minute eclipse-viewing glasses. It was hard not to get caught up in the excitement. How long would it last? Would it look like nighttime? Would Iggy finally start to talk?

The kennel staff was an extremely focused, hardworking group, and so I was not surprised that the imminent total eclipse was not the topic on everyone's lips. As a weekly volunteer I understood the limitations of my role, meaning it was not my place to burst through the door shouting, *"Are we excited about the eclipse?"* Of course Axel knew about the coast-to-coast celestial event that comes around only every century or so. Did I bludgeon him with information, trying to get him to share my fervor? Perhaps. That afternoon I worked with him and one of his friends to turn cereal boxes into eclipse viewers, and we stood outside in the backyard to wait for the magic. The boys were good sports, but they were...boys. Once they saw that the sun wasn't actually exploding and sending balls of fire down onto our street, they lost interest. Even I had to admit that the whole thing was a tad underwhelming, given the frenzied lead-up and my lack of proper viewing glasses. But what was missing was not the drama of the eclipse itself. It was the drama surrounding it that I longed to share.

And that's when I felt it fully: I really missed my office.

Perhaps, Searching in San Francisco, you and I are different. Perhaps the routine of being in your house much of the time, with a dog and a boy as your companions, will not begin to feel tedious. But it had for me, and the eclipse was the tipping point.

Why do we go to work? Oh, there are too many reasons to count, most of them practical, beginning with the need to make money to put food on the table. But it's the silly reasons that often make the work great. Once while the three of us were watching an episode of *The Office,* my husband turned to Axel and said, "You know, that's not really what work is like." I suppose it's not. But to spend your days with energetic, inquisitive people who understand that sometimes you must stop working for most of the day when there is a significant astronomical occurrence because there's so much to talk about? Bliss. My former workplace was populated by fascinating and occasionally ridiculous people who believed that life should be filled with awe-inspiring and spectacular events that can make you miss an entire day of work. Maybe your old office was not like that, Searching—not fun. But I ask you: Is that too much to want?

(8) Finally: Wait

When you are in a longtime career that ends abruptly, whether because you are laid off in a round of budget cuts or because you quit in a huff, your primary goal is just to get out of there alive, like you are abandoning a sinking ship. At first you bob along feeling so lucky to have landed in a lifeboat. The sun is beautiful and the sea is relatively calm, and although there may be worry and uncertainty, you're also ecstatic that you're finally free. You look at your water and food supply and know that you have enough to last until fate intervenes to rescue you, because surely fate will intervene, as it always has. And so you wait. Perhaps you get a little bored, but you are so glad that you are off that big ship where you were just going to die anyway. You wait a bit longer. Eventually something will come along to save you, you're sure of it.

Then the bright sun begins to feel punishing, and you realize you actually have no idea where you are. Why didn't you think to bring a compass to navigate this limitless, unfamiliar world? Or is what you actually need called a sextant? Why didn't you learn details like that before you left the ship? Big, powerful ocean liners zoom past you. Bright, happy sailboats skim by. Immense container vessels appear on the horizon, loom taller than skyscrapers, and leave you struggling in their wake. They all have someplace important to go, and no one stops for you. In fact, you're certain that no one sees you at all. You begin to wonder whether your lifeboat promises not freedom and salvation but increasing boredom and, quite possibly, death.

You become lonely and scared.

And then you think to yourself, *Oh my God, I've got to get off this fucking lifeboat.*

My dear Searching in San Francisco, you will not be on the lifeboat forever. Already you have learned so much. Maybe this period is not what you imagined; maybe the lifeboat is a lot lonelier than you expected; maybe you've discovered things about yourself that you would rather not know. But you will be fine. You were fine—more than fine—for fifty years, and you will be fine again.

With best wishes for your future,
Kristin

Chapter 18
My Fratermily

When you live in a fraternity, there is a certain code of conduct that members must follow, or so I imagine. For example, if you are playing Call of Duty in your room, you wear headphones with a clever attached microphone so that when you shout at your fellow gamers, you're just quiet enough that the person in the next bedroom can hear you but can't actually make out the words. That way, if you are keeping that person awake, instead of lying in bed stewing about the fact that it's after midnight and she has to rise at seven a.m. to don a mask and wait in line to get into Stop and Shop, she can lie there trying to figure out what exactly it is you're saying, which is much more stimulating, from a mental-exercise perspective.

When you live in a fraternity and leave a skillet encrusted with the remains of your grilled cheese sandwich on the stove, you should wait to see if one of your brothers or the house manager will step in and clean it, because after all you are a team and they know that you "always forget."

When you live in a fraternity and the bathroom becomes incredibly dirty and smells like a latrine used by a platoon of blind soldiers who pee eighteen times a day, that is definitely not your fault, your problem, or your responsibility to fix.

In a fraternity, of course the dogs sleep on the sofa with the white slipcover and in bed with you on top of your white sheets and white duvet and it doesn't matter that they are black Labs who shed more and more as spring advances because honestly, in the grand scheme of things, who cares?

If there is one Tate's chocolate chip cookie left in the Costco-size box in the fraternity pantry, you may eat the cookie but you must leave the box there; that way the person responsible for buying cookies, whoever she is, will see the empty box and know that she needs to get more. The same rule applies to ice cream bars, instant oatmeal, and strawberries that come in clear plastic containers. Best to leave the empty packaging where it is so the buyer person can see it. Makes her life easier.

The key to living in a fraternity, it seems, is to never lift a finger, always shift the blame, eat whenever you can, drink as much as possible. Most important of all, you must pretend you're having a good time, even when you're not. After experiencing social distancing, I've found that the same holds true for a family, particularly if that family consists of middle-aged parents and three boys crammed together under one roof by a coronavirus pandemic for an indefinite period for the first time in many years. What had been a calm, somewhat organized home has become—in just a few weeks—a fraternity, one where the members all happen to be related. A *fratermily,* if you will. The meal plan is in shambles, the cleaning schedule has flown out the window, and our chapter has been placed on probation, meaning Governor Andrew Cuomo locked the doors from the outside.

The world has suffered a global tragedy, and my family members and I have nothing to complain about. Everyone is healthy, and if the dogs are sick, they're keeping it to themselves. I am not a doctor or a nurse, the governor of a state or the mayor of any kind of municipality. And while I'm down to my last roll of paper towels, I have plenty of toilet paper, not to mention two giant bags of quinoa from Costco that I've been meaning to use up anyway.

But even the hale and lucky among us must make small, unpleasant adjustments. My son Hugo is twenty-one, and this is his final semester of college. According to breaking news from the president of his university, Hugo will have a "virtual" graduation ceremony; as his mother, I try not to dwell on the fact that the word *virtual* has several meanings, as we're still not entirely sure he fixed that missing-half-a-credit thing. This man-child spent the last three years of college living in a real fraternity, which is where he would so much rather be now. I suppose I should feel happy that the house Hugo shares with me is not nearly as disgusting as the house he lives in on campus, where your feet stick to the floor as you walk from room to room and every surface smells like beer. Even if you take the boy out of the fraternity, however, you can't take the fraternity completely out of the boy. Two nights ago my husband and I were walking down the stairs at eleven and Hugo walked past us, balancing a plate piled high with scrambled eggs. Of course he had eaten dinner, but that had been a full four hours earlier.

"Wow," I said after he passed. "It's like...it's like..."

"It's like a plague of locusts," my husband said.

Recently Hugo saw on Twitter—that balanced source of important news and pet videos—that because of the coronavirus pandemic, there were now only three days of the week: yesterday, today, and tomorrow. This is so true! Yesterday was the day I cleaned the microwave, today is the day someone reheats Bolognese sauce and it splatters all over the inside of the microwave, and tomorrow is the day I start yelling, "Would you all please, for the love of God, clean the inside of the microwave when your lunch explodes?" Although sometimes I'm yelling about the bathroom sink, or the muddy stairs, or the half-eaten bowl of cereal that's been on the bench in the upstairs hall since two yesterdays ago.

Like the word *virtual, fraternity* has several meanings. I can't say we are a group of people who share common interests, as my interests (quietness, order, evenly distributed domestic duties) are in direct opposition to those of my three sons (sleeping till noon, arguing about whose turn it is to take out the recycling, dribbling the basketball in the kitchen while Mom is on a Zoom call). But there are moments, sweet moments, when we five exist in a state of something that feels like friendship. Moments we actually laugh together, like when our dog Jill has a little white feather stuck in the fur on top of her head, right above her eyes, and she doesn't know it's there.

But remember the scene in *It's a Wonderful Life* when George Bailey asks, "Why do we have to have all these kids?" I asked my husband the same thing the other day. It seemed like such a good idea at the time, when they were little and cuter and my husband and I were young and cared more.

Times like these can make it impossible to know who your true friends are. Apparently this worldwide crisis has led certain people to trust the media even less than they did, which, as someone who works in the media and is married to someone who works in the media, I ought to take personally. But I get it. The media is definitely not on our side here. Although the coverage of the pandemic is not the problem. It's the "helpful" exhortations from all of my favorite papers, magazines, and websites and their cheerful lists of all the wholesome ways I can use this time together with my youngest son, Axel. We can watch the giant panda cam at the Atlanta Zoo and then learn everything there is to know about giant pandas! Or visit the MIT something-something to learn how to do something, maybe write code, I don't remember. Or do puzzles. Puzzles! Axel is thirteen and he hates puzzles. He hates everything but watching *Parks and Rec* and playing Fortnite, and those two pursuits occupy most of his now-abundant free time. It's a parenting riddle: Do I keep the peace by letting him watch eight episodes of *Parks and Rec* in one day, or do I become a "good parent" and force him to join me in assembling the thousand-piece puzzle that has been sitting on our dining-room table for the better part of the week, the one with the photograph of the football stadium at the university that may or may not be giving his older brother a diploma in a month? And if I'm doing the puzzle with Axel, when will I have time to watch *Unorthodox*? Because right now Netflix is putting a lot of pressure on me with so many good shows and only three days in the week in which to watch them.

Yes, the unspoken message from some experts seems to be that if I don't pay close attention to the panda cam or write code or do thousand-piece puzzles of football stadiums, I'm a lazy person and very bad parent. And yet there are other experts telling me that now is the time to let myself off the hook. Practice self-care. Slow down. Give my mind, body, and spirit a break. It's all so confusing! Am I supposed to be making myself, my family, and my world better, one annoying wholesome pursuit at a time, or should I be staring out the kitchen window at the squirrel who has learned that if he hangs upside down and holds on for dear life, he can eat all of the birdseed in the feeder that I forgot I owned until I tripped over it one day when I was wandering around in my garage?

Was I wandering around in the garage during the abundant free time the internet now says I have? Hmmm. Technically speaking, I have indeed "gained" the two hours per day I would otherwise have spent commuting to and from work. Two hours! That sounds like a lot of time and, in other hands, it might actually be put to good use. If you believe Facebook, people all over the world are making sourdough starter and memorizing "The Owl and the Pussycat" so they can stand up and recite it for their family members at dinner. They are meditating and growing tomato plants from seed and learning to play classical guitar, all of this during the time they would otherwise have spent commuting to and from work. And me? I am tripping over things in the garage and planning the next meal. In the words of Nora Ephron, "I don't think any day is worth living without thinking about what you're going to eat next at all times." I know exactly what she meant, except when it comes from her, it sounds like fun. But just as a gas will expand to fit the shape of its container, my family's need for food expands to fit the amount of time I have to wait on them hand and foot. And no matter how often I feed them, time marches on and before you can say, "Who ate the rest of the mozzarella?" I have to feed them again. So there you have it, internet—there's my extra two hours.

A few weeks ago, Gwyneth Paltrow caused a small national panic by saying that we all should be writing novels during this pandemic, but she isn't the only one with insane suggestions. Every night the superintendent of schools in my little suburban town sends a COVID-19 update e-mail. It was once required reading in my household, back in the early days of self-isolation when she would mention the number of confirmed cases in our district. But that number has now grown so large that someone higher up the municipal food chain decided it's better for the taxpayers not to know. If you don't fall down the Facebook rabbit hole of parents with opinions about how our schools should be run (and that is a particularly dark and scary rabbit hole, its walls lined with thorns) but instead just ask me, a truly shitty homeschooler and disinterested mom, I will tell you that our superintendent is doing a wonderful job. I'm not exactly sure what her role normally entails—I know she has to attend the homecoming football game, for example, and say a few words at high-school graduation—but now she must figure out how her teachers can pull off remote learning (while homeschooling their own children; try to wrap your head around that), plus provide free meals for the families who rely on them, plus turn one of our elementary schools into a day-care center for first responders' kids. It's a lot to handle, and I'm sincerely grateful for her steady, dedicated leadership.

But her e-mail from last night—with the subject line *Wednesday's COVID-19 Update*—cast a slight shadow over my estimation of her, because she has joined Goop and Facebook and even my beloved *New York Times* in providing me with a list of exhausting activities I can suggest to Axel that he will immediately, and strenuously, resist. I don't even have to show him the list; I already know how he will respond:

- read independently or listen to an audiobook ["Or watch *Parks and Rec*"]
- listen to a podcast or watch a documentary ["Or there's Fortnite"]
- do a puzzle or word search ["Everybody hates puzzles, duh"]
- write a story or keep a journal ["Writing is boring"; "What's a journal?"]
- draw a map of your neighborhood ["Why?"]
- dance ["Noob!"]
- exercise ["Does basketball in the kitchen equal exercise?"]
- stretch, do yoga, meditate ["As if"; cf. *boys*]

- work in the garden ["That's what moms do"]
- listen to music ["Mom hates all our music except that dumb seventies Soul Essentials playlist on iTunes"]
- color, draw, paint [see "As if," above]
- write a letter to someone special ["What's a letter?" plus "Define *special*"]
- build a fort and tell stories in it ["Will Byers built an amazing fort in *Stranger Things* and we all know what happened to him"]

So now I must question all of the media plus our school superintendent. Oh, and Google Calendar, with its methodical reminders that today is the day that spring soccer starts, or my boot-camp class is set to begin in fifteen minutes, or Axel has a seven p.m. lacrosse game. Screw you, Google Calendar. There was a time when you were helpful; now you're just making me feel bad.

One thing that no doubt distinguishes a bona fide fraternity from a slapdash fratermily is the amount of public crying, and it's not just at my house. My friend Courtney told me that these days she cries every afternoon, and the strangest things can invite tears, like when her favorite pharmacist thoughtfully called to ask whether she needed a prescription refilled. I don't have a thoughtful favorite pharmacist, and perhaps that fact alone should make me cry. But I do find my eyes welling up at unexpected times, like when I was online and happened upon Randy Rainbow performing the Tom Waits song "Martha" in a scene I didn't understand from a TV show I don't watch. Or when my friend Heather and I were taking a walk and were affronted by this persistent, God-awful honking, only to discover that it was the teachers from the local elementary school driving parade-style through the streets. They had signs attached to their cars and were calling out the windows to students who had run onto the sidewalk when they heard the racket. I saw my family's all-time-favorite teacher, Mrs. Rossi, and I blew her a kiss, tears streaming down my face. There aren't many occasions when the moment I'm living looks like a viral video, and I was quite disappointed that Lester Holt didn't show a clip of our little honking car parade on the next *NBC Nightly News.* You know, at the end of the show when, after half an hour of terrifying reports, the producers allow him forty-five seconds to tell a heartwarming story. Note to NBC: This pandemic calls for a sweet story at the top of the show too.

We must embrace the moments of hope when we can, like the forgotten bird feeder I found in my garage. I dragged it out and hung it up and now I look at it throughout the day and it makes me happy, at least when the squirrel has had his fill and the chickadee gets a turn. Not everyone lives in a fratermily, but we're all members of a fraternity of humans who have to get up every day and try to do our best with what remains. I may not be able to do a jigsaw puzzle. But when Lester ends his broadcast by telling me to take care of myself and others, I think, *I can do that.* And so I turn off the TV and go searching for my family, because I'm sure it's time to give them something to eat.

Chapter 19

Letter of Apology to a Son Graduating from College

Dear Owen,

Well, here we are. In just a few weeks you will graduate from college. Many things have happened over the
past four years; the biggest is that while I was looking
the other way, you became a man—someone who can
drink and vote and die for our country. (I know you
do the first two; I hope you never do the last.)

You're wrapping up your college years writing your thesis (puzzles in the work of Emily Dickinson), and I'm wrapping up your college years cataloging my regrets (puzzles in the work of motherhood). When I was your age, a writing teacher told me that everything funny is a little bit sad, and everything sad is a little bit funny. For some reason this keeps coming back to me as I think about your graduation. Maybe every joy carries a bit of regret.

Remember the summer after fifth grade when we went to Target a month before the start of middle school and bought all the supplies you would need, including a lock for your locker? Having a locker—and being able to manage a combination lock—was such a big deal! You had your school supplies in hand well in advance, so I thought you were prepared. And then you misplaced half the supplies in the landfill that was your bedroom. So on the last day of summer vacation, I had a nine p.m., history-making Mom Freak-Out. Where were the notebooks? Where were the pencils? Where was the lock for your locker? You sat cross-legged on the floor, your skinny frame surrounded by half-full Target bags, and silently began to cry. In that moment I failed you completely.

The hardest part of parenting is knowing when to step in and when to step back. You are still absentminded.

(Remember spring break 2017, when your wallet was "lost" in the car for two days?) I have learned, however, that you always find your way. Combination locks! Who. Cares. But you see, my (over)reaction that night had nothing to do with whether you had all your supplies and everything to do with wanting to feel that I had life under control as you entered the uncharted world of combination locks and cell phones and walking to school every day with a friend instead of a parent.

So I apologize for that, and for all the other times when I took my issues and made them yours.

I apologize, too, for the times I co-opted your triumphs. Perhaps this is true of all parents, but one of my greatest mistakes as a mother was to conflate your success with mine. Every accomplishment of yours meant less working-mom guilt for me. If you got an A on a test, I gave myself an A; if you made the varsity team, so did I. I was raised by a loving stay-at-home mom, and by working full-time when you were growing up, I feared you would be less smart, less happy, less emotionally sound. (Turns out that was me.)

I'm sorry I didn't pay more attention, didn't write down every single thing you said in a notebook while you were still the little boy who would crawl into bed with me and say, "Let's hold hands." The boy who wanted nothing more than to be by my side, before you became an overscheduled teenager and then a polite young man who has learned how to gracefully deflect a prying parent. I know that little boy is still in there somewhere, and I know this is the natural order of things. But now you are like an Emily Dickinson poem: beautiful, brilliant, mysterious.

I have taught you many things: how to ask for what you need; how to silence distraction when it's time to focus; how to water a plant, write a thank-you note, iron a shirt, comfort a friend (or a mother). But you have taught me much more. I now know, for example, what *bougie* means. And I think I know how to let go.

Years ago I read a parenting book that included this advice: When your child does something amazing, do not say, "I am so proud of you." Instead say, "You should feel so proud of yourself." That is a hard habit to break, inserting the parental *I* and confusing your child's identity with your own. Forgetting that it's not about you. Stepping in when you should be stepping back. And so I will say to you, Owen, on the day you don that cap and gown: My beloved child, you should feel so proud of yourself. It was all you.

Love,
Mom

Chapter 20
Things

Things That Aren't Worth It:

- cleaning the oven more than once a year
- dunking the vegetables in an ice bath
- carrying a big purse. In fact, carrying any kind of purse, if you can put Blistex in your pocket and your credit card in your phone case.
- arguing with your sixteen-year-old about whether he needs to put on his winter coat
- worrying that anyone is looking at you in a communal changing room

- wondering if there's something better out there when you are already happy enough
- trying to open clamshell packaging without using scissors
- holding a grudge
- making the kid clean his plate
- chopping fresh thyme leaves, even if the recipe calls for it. Just do your best to get them off the stems and throw them in the pot.
- a bread maker
- high-waisted jeans, unless you are under thirty or stick-thin
- taking twenty minutes to make scrambled eggs, even if Julia Child did it that way
- ironing the tablecloth. Just put it on the table, mist it with water, and wait an hour. I swear this works.

Things That Are Annoying but Unavoidable:

- needing your reading glasses to make dinner
- needing a magnifying glass to figure out how to launder your new shirt
- Spandex
- packing, for any kind of trip, even if it's just one night
- Facebook

Things That Will Always Be Confusing:

- how much to tip
- Bitcoin
- how anybody can fall asleep on a train
- whether saying "God bless you" when a stranger sneezes is polite or an invasion of privacy
- how sometimes the leaves of the plant turn yellow because you are underwatering, and sometimes they turn yellow because you are overwatering
- why the cat always wants to sit in the lap of the person who hates cats
- how much of the scallion to use in the recipe
- how you can parent two children exactly the same way and they turn out completely different
- why your hands are always cold

Things You Are Better Off Not Thinking About:

- the fact that if you understood all of the features on your iPhone, your life might improve by 25 percent
- how you could have been a better parent
- whether, at a certain point, you will become too old to wear shorts

- death, unless it's to make a list of the songs you want someone to play at your funeral

Things You Learn Along the Way:

- tomatoes and butter must be kept out of the refrigerator
- one more dog usually makes things better
- it is not impossible, although it's quite difficult, to love a novel even if you hate all of the characters
- just showing up for work on time every day puts you ahead of a lot of people
- two-in-one shampoo/conditioner is basically just shampoo
- the day will come when simply being in the front passenger seat makes you nervous, because everyone who is not you drives too fast
- the answer to nearly all of life's questions is "It depends"
- the instant one child gets himself straightened out, the next one does something to worry you
- When a friend is getting divorced, it's best to keep your views to yourself unless you are asked. And even then, watch out.

- Some words are so stupid, you should never say them out loud. *Eatery,* for example.
- eventually you will have too many scented candles
- there are certain people you will never win over, no matter how hard you try
- breakfast like a king, lunch like a prince, dinner like a pauper
- reality TV is rarely worth it
- when it comes to paper towels and paper napkins, you get what you pay for
- you reach an age when Eileen Fisher is no longer the punchline of a joke
- When someone says, "I love you," the only kind response is "I love you too." Do not overthink it.
- even if you live to be a hundred, you will never meet anyone who has actually slipped on a banana peel

And, Finally, One Thing from Anton Chekhov:

"We must not forget that the newer the year, the closer to death, the more extensive the bald spot, the more sinuous the wrinkles." You can look at this two ways. The first way: Death, bald spot, wrinkles. The better way: It may have taken decades, but finally someone has described you as *sinuous.*

Acknowledgments

Thank you to Richard Pine, who told me I should write this book. Richard, it turns out that you were right. As you are about most things. Except coffee, obviously.

Thanks to Tracy Behar, dream editor, who once again saw the path connecting "Kristin's Random Grab Bag of Dopey Ideas" to "Book." Not only do you have that supportive, gentle touch, but you are much smarter than I am, without making me feel bad about myself. So double thanks for that.

Gregg Kulick, thank you for the hilarious perfect cover and the charming perfect illustrations and for letting me bug you so many times about the dog collar.

Thank you to the excellent team at Little, Brown, including but not limited to Ian Straus, Jayne Yaffe Kemp, Tracy Roe, Gail Cohen, Carolyn Levin, Jessica Chun, and Elizabeth Garriga.

To the wonderful friends and coworkers who allowed me to borrow stories, experiences, and wisdom from their lives and write about them in this book. (Is it borrowing, or actually stealing? Still not sure.)

To Nandini Anandu and Miguel Silva, who quite possibly prevented me from dying of sepsis.

Thanks to Susannah Schrobsdorff, who edited the pieces that first appeared in *Time,* and Annie Stoltie, who edited "Rebel Love" for *Adirondack Life.*

Thanks to the staff of *Real Simple,* circa 2016. Hopefully now you understand why I always looked tired. And to my InkWell colleagues, particularly those who didn't allow their eyes to glaze over as I talked about this book. (Looking at you, David and Jessie.)

Acknowledgments

Thanks to Jenny, Kay, and Glen Robinson for their unconditional support and love for the last thirty-five (!) years.

To my sisters, Valerie and Claire, for understanding just about everything.

To Dean, Owen, Hugo, and Axel, who simultaneously cared and—if we're being honest—didn't care at all that I was writing another book in which they featured prominently.

To my mother, Connie van Ogtrop, for an A+ kind of calm, good-natured, non-judgy parenting that I am still trying to perfect.

And to my father, Piet Hein van Ogtrop, for always thinking I'm funnier than I actually am.

About the Author

Kristin van Ogtrop is a literary agent at InkWell Management. In her previous life, she wrote a column called the Amateur for *Time,* was the editor in chief of *Real Simple*, and was named by *Fortune* as one of the "55 Most Influential Women on Twitter," a designation she now finds absurd. She was a contributor to the *New York Times* bestseller *The Bitch in the House* and the author of *Just Let Me Lie Down: Necessary Terms for the Half-Insane Working Mom*. She lives in Westchester County, New York, with her husband, two dogs, and any number of children, depending on the day.

instagram.com/kvanogtrop
twitter.com/kvanogtrop
kristinvanogtrop.com